Effective Communication Skills

Essential Skills for Success in Work and Life
Second Edition

Marsha Ludden

Effective Communication Skills, **Second Edition**
Essential Skills for Success in Work and Life

Published by JIST Works, an imprint of JIST Publishing, Inc.
8902 Otis Avenue
Indianapolis, IN 46216-1033

Phone: 1-800-648-JIST   Fax: 1-800-JIST-FAX
E-mail: info@jist.com   Web site: www.jist.com

Note to instructors. A thorough instructor's guide and a related video support this book. Call 1-800-648-JIST or visit www.jist.com for details.

About career materials published by JIST. Our materials encourage people to be self-directed and to take control of their destinies. We work hard to provide excellent content, solid advice, and techniques that get results. If you have questions about this book or other JIST products, call 1-800-648-JIST or visit www.jist.com.

Quantity discounts are available for JIST products. Call 1-800-648-JIST or visit www.jist.com for a free catalog and for more information.

Visit www.jist.com. Find out about our products, get free book chapters, order a catalog, and link to other career-related sites. You can also learn more about JIST authors and JIST training available to professionals.

Acquisitions Editor: Lori Cates Hand
Development Editor: Mary Ellen Stephenson
Cover Designer: Aleata Howard
Page Layout Coordinator: Carolyn J. Newland
Proofreader: Jeanne Clark

Printed in the United States of America

06 05 04 03 02 01   9 8 7 6 5 4 3 2 1

We have been careful to provide accurate information throughout this book, but it is possible that errors and omissions have been introduced. Please consider this in making any career plans or other important decisions. Trust your own judgment above all else and in all things.

ISBN 1-56370-852-3

About This Book

Effective Communication Skills has been written to encourage you to use communication skills in the classroom as well as in your daily life. It can help you

- Become aware of the importance of communication in both work and social situations

- Understand that communicating is done with both words and wordless messages

- Practice this valuable life skill in an informal group situation

- Learn how to use the latest electronic communication media, including e-mail, cell phones, voice mail, faxes, and pagers

You'll see sample conversations, letters, and phone messages in the book, drawn from real-life situations. The "Check It Out" exercises will help sharpen your reading and writing skills, as well as your ability to evaluate situations calling for clear communication.

Contents

Chapter 4

Communicating Over the Telephone 45

Chapter 5

Messages Without Words 67

Chapter 6

Written Communication 79

Chapter 7

Chapter 8

Introduction

The alarm goes off at 6 a.m. A highly charged disk jockey greets you with "Good morning!!! It is six o'clock at WCOM. Time to stretch those tired muscles."

Before your body has even risen from your warm bed, two ideas run through your mind.

Number one: "I need to get up."

Number two: "I shouldn't have watched the late, late show last night."

With a few moans and groans, you manage to stumble to the bathroom. After brushing, washing, and combing, you head for the kitchen. While reading the morning newspaper, you crunch a bowl of Crispy Cracklers cereal. An ad in the newspaper reads:

Before breakfast is over, two more ideas have entered your head.

Number one: "Forget these soggy Crispy Cracklers. I want fresh bagels."

Number two: "I would look great at the big game this weekend if I could get a new sweater."

Without further thought, you head off for Hugo's House of Bargains. Having loaded up on bagels and purchased the perfect sweater, you arrive at your job. As you start to check your e-mail, you notice a sticky note attached to the monitor. Written in red ink, the note reads, "You are late. Report to me immediately." Your supervisor has signed it. Again two ideas form in your mind.

Number one: "I am in trouble."

Number two: "I wonder what size sweater my supervisor wears."

You receive messages constantly. Some are written, like the newspaper ad and the office note. Some are computer driven, like your e-mail. Others are spoken, like the radio disk jockey's morning chatter. Some, like the red ink, are silent messages.

You send messages as well as receive them. You wave to a neighbor as you take out the garbage, and a message is sent. You open your mouth and speak, and a message is sent. You write a note to a coworker, and a message is sent. You answer the telephone, and a message is sent. Each contact demonstrates a different way of communicating.

Communication is simply sending and receiving messages. This book deals with all kinds of messages. It will teach you how to send clear messages and how to understand the messages that you receive.

CHAPTER 1

What Is Communication?

Communication is a sharing of thoughts among people. At least two people must be involved for communication to take place. Speaking is verbal communication. Nonverbal communication may use written messages and both body movements and facial expressions. As messengers share their thoughts, listeners interpret the message they receive. In a conversation, people take turns being messengers and receivers. Communication is what you think other people are telling you. Communication is also what other people think you are telling them.

Check It Out   1-1

Read the following situations. Find the messages being sent.

Situation No. 1: Following a meeting with her supervisor, Tasha slams the door as she enters the breakroom. She throws her file folder and pen on the table, where Nick, a co-worker, is reading a magazine. Nick smiles and asks, "How did the meeting go?" Without saying a word, Tasha stomps out of the room, slamming the door behind her.

1. What message is Tasha sending Nick? _____

    _____

    _____

    _____

2. What message is Nick sending Tasha? _____

    _____

    _____

    _____

Now read a second situation; a few actions have changed. What messages are being sent this time?

Situation No. 2: Following a meeting with her supervisor, Tasha enters the breakroom. She throws her file folder and pen on the table, where Nick, a co-worker, is reading a magazine. She smiles at him as she grabs a cool drink from the refrigerator. Nick's eyes never leave the magazine. Without saying a word, Tasha stomps out of the room, slamming the door behind her.

3. What message is Tasha sending Nick? _____

    _____

    _____

    _____

4. What message is Nick sending Tasha? _____

    _____

    _____

    _____

    _____

Tasha and Nick have each communicated with the other. The messages that they sent reflected their thoughts, attitudes, and emotions. In each situation, Nick and Tasha have been both a messenger and a receiver.

Nick and Tasha used few words to communicate. Communication doesn't always involve spoken words. In the exercise, Nick and Tasha sent messages through body action, facial expressions, and eye contact—all types of nonverbal, or unspoken, communication.

If you want to avoid communicating with others, you can seal yourself up in a box. However, someone will probably come along, knock on the box, and ask, "What are you doing in there?" When you refuse to answer, your nonverbal message will say to them, "Go away! I want to be alone."

You're stuck! You can't avoid communication. But you can learn to communicate well to help you get ahead in life.

Good Communication Skills Lead to Success

The development of good communication skills is essential to your success in life. You can't escape communicating with those around you. Whether you speak or not, you send messages to everyone you meet. Others will evaluate you by the way you communicate. If you can express your ideas to others, they will see you in a positive way.

Your communication skills affect your self-confidence. Have you ever found yourself remembering a conversation you had with another person? Perhaps you thought of all the things you wish you had said. The longer you think about the conversation, the more ill at ease you feel. You begin to see yourself as inadequate.

Some Problems from Poor Communication

Poor communication can lead to misunderstandings with other people. Without clear communication, you and your date could arrive at a formal office party in jeans and T-shirts. Poor communication of a customer's order could cost that customer's business. Poor communication could leave the boss's wife waiting at the airport while you look for her at the train station. Poor communication could mean that you are scheduled to work all weekend because you failed to ask your supervisor for time off.

Poor communication also affects your ability to get a job. A report published by several U.S. government agencies, called *21st Century Skills for 21st Century Jobs*, lists communication among the skills sought by today's employers. The person who speaks in a clear, confident manner will impress an employer. The person who looks at the floor and mumbles will give a negative impression and seem to lack the ability to do the job. If you were an employer, which person would you hire?

Poor communication affects your ability to keep a job. An employee who can't accurately relay a telephone message could cost the business time and money. A store employee who doesn't respond to a customer's annoyed facial expression could lose a sale. A waiter's inability to write an order clearly for the chef could result in the wrong meal being prepared. An employer would find such poor communication skills unacceptable.

Business leaders estimate that they lose millions of dollars each year due to poor communication by employees. Businesses operate to make money. If a business loses more money than it makes, it will be forced to close. An employee who causes a business to lose money won't have a job for very long.

Check it Out 1-2

Fill in the sentence blanks using the word bank below. Do not use any word twice.

communication	conversation	negative
evaluate	nonverbal	verbal
employees	sending	impress
job	unacceptable	receiving
self-confidence	millions	speak

1. Speaking is _____ communication.

2. In a _____, people take turns being messengers and receivers.

3. When a speaker looks at the floor and mumbles, the listener gets a _____ impression of that person.

4. Poor communication results in the loss of _____ of dollars to businesses each year.

5. Body action, facial expressions, and eye contact are _____ ways in which people communicate.

6. _____ is a sharing of thoughts and ideas.

7. In a job interview, a person who speaks clearly will _____ the interviewer.

8. Communicating means _____ messages to other people.

9. Communicating also means _____ messages from other people.

10. Others will _____ you by the way you speak.

11. You will have more _____ if you can make other people understand your thoughts.

12. Poor communication skills are _____ to an employer.

13. Employers look for _____ with good communication skills.

14. Employees who cannot communicate well might not be able to keep a _____.

15. Even when you don't _____, you send messages to others.

Different Forms of Communication

Communication takes many different forms. Reading, writing, and speaking are most commonly associated with communicating.

Speaking words is called verbal communication. The average person communicates through speech about 23 percent of the time.

Yet the average person listens to communication about 53 percent of the time. Clearly, we listen a lot more than we speak, but most people fail to see listening as a communication skill. Listening is possibly the most neglected communication skill, even though we use it the most. Recognizing the importance of listening can greatly enhance the communication process.

Sometimes, communication is nonverbal. This means that no words are spoken. Actions can express the person's thoughts. Such actions include a football player spiking the ball after a touchdown, a child crying when her helium balloon escapes her grasp, or a motorist tailgating a slower car on the highway.

We call this nonverbal communication body language. A person's posture, facial expressions, hand gestures, and eye contact with another individual send messages to that person.

Other forms of nonverbal communication include reading and writing. The average person communicates by reading messages 13.3 percent of the time. Communicating by writing messages, including letters, notes, and memos, occurs only 8.4 percent of the time.

With recent advancements in technology, machines have had an effect on the world of communication. Sending and receiving messages through the telephone, the computer, and the fax machine has become a part of our daily lives. Many people check personal and business e-mail (electronic mail) daily. Many enterprises have grown so dependent upon machines for communicating that a power outage forces them to close.

Check It Out   1-3

You use different types of communication each day. Think about the different ways that people communicate. Give examples of different types of communication and the situations that call for each type of communication.

List three examples of verbal communication:

1. _____
2. _____
3. _____

List three situations where listening skills are needed:

1. _____
2. _____
3. _____

List three examples of nonverbal communication:

1. _____
2. _____
3. _____

List three examples of written communication:

1. _____
2. _____
3. _____

List three ways of communicating using technological means:

1. _____
2. _____
3. _____

Communication Is a Learned Activity

Communication is not a quickly acquired skill. You gradually learned to communicate through everyday life. Your family and your friends contributed to your communication skills. You have had experiences that have influenced the way you communicate.

Some early childhood educators believe that communication occurs before birth. Some parents play certain types of music or read to an unborn child, believing that such communication can raise the child's intelligence. Research has not proven that this works; however, it does suggest that communication may begin before birth.

Voices mean a lot in a newborn's life. The baby recognizes the voices of mother and father and other family members. If an infant hears a strange voice, he will often react unpleasantly.

Baby talk begins as an infant mimics sounds he or she hears. At first, the talk is merely gurgling and cooing. Later, "words" become a part of baby talk. Often these sounds aren't clear adult language, but verbal communication has started. Over time, the child's use of language increases. Words become phrases. Finally, the child puts these words and phrases together to form complete sentences. When a child can express his thoughts to someone else, he accomplishes verbal communication.

How Language Develops

A child who has been talked to and asked questions develops language skills earlier in life than one who wasn't talked to. The amount of communication in your childhood home has affected your ability to participate in conversation. If you grew up in a home where English was not spoken as the first language, you may have experienced some difficulty communicating in our society. If your parent had a speech problem, such as stuttering, you might have developed the same problem.

Family experiences affect your vocabulary. Your family might consider certain phrases or words to be vulgar or unacceptable. As a result, you might react negatively if you hear someone use them in a conversation. Your vocabulary may include colloquialisms, that is, words with special meanings in certain regions of the country. If you move to another region of the country, those words may have a totally different meaning.

Some families or groups have a secret language that has a special meaning for them. One family of all boys uses the term "Geronimo!" to let one of the guys know that his fly is open. Using their secret word, they avoid embarrassment in public. Nicknames may also be considered part of a secret language. Perhaps some special early happening resulted in you gaining a nickname, but people not familiar with your family history might not understand your connection to the nickname.

As you became older, friends entered your life. They also influenced your verbal communication. Friends often use slang around each other. By using common English words and giving them new meanings, you and your friends may have developed a "slang language" that your family did not understand.

Within your family unit, you also learned about nonverbal communication. If you were punished for stomping your foot or slamming a door, you learned that such nonverbal communication was not acceptable. Physical contact within a family is another way of communicating. In some families, a "bear" hug shows affection. Other families may not be comfortable with such close contact. You probably learned to "read" facial expressions. By observing mother's face, even a small child knows whether she is angry or happy. Young children sometimes ask, "Why do you have a sad face?"

Friends also influenced your understanding of nonverbal communication. As a toddler, you communicated using physical contact. Since you could not tell your friend that you had no intention of sharing your toy, you probably resorted to hair pulling, pushing, or biting. These forms of nonverbal communication simply said, "I am not sharing with you."

As you grew older, you learned to use hand gestures and body language in communicating. You learned to use not only your ears to hear what your friends were saying, but also your eyes to interpret their meaning.

Your school experiences affected the development of your communication skills. Listening became a very important skill to use. When a teacher gave instructions, your attention needed to be focused on listening. Staring out the window or drumming your fingers on the desk were unacceptable forms of nonverbal communication. A teacher exercised control over the amount of verbal and nonverbal communication that took place in the classroom. She set a time to speak and a time to listen.

Check It Out   **1-4**

The way you communicate has been influenced by your family, your friends, and your school and life experiences. Think about these influences, and answer the following questions.

1. Name one way that your family has influenced your communication skills.

    _____
    _____
    _____

2. Was this a positive or negative influence? Why? _____

    _____
    _____
    _____

3. Name one way that your friends have influenced your communication skills.

    _____
    _____
    _____

4. Was this a positive or negative influence? Why? _____

    _____
    _____
    _____

5. Name one way that your school experiences have influenced your communication skills. _____

    _____
    _____
    _____

6. Was this a positive or negative influence? Why? _____

    _____
    _____
    _____

Communication in the Workplace

Employers look for people who can communicate well. Speaking clearly when using the telephone or talking to customers is vital. Slang may be fine with your friends, but employers expect the proper use of English. Plus, many businesses operate worldwide. Speaking both English and other languages is a valuable business skill.

Jargon is the special language used by workers in their job situation. For example, to a nurse "prepping" means to get a patient ready for surgery. To a picture framer "prepping" means to stretch the canvas before it can be put into a frame. To a teacher "prepping" means writing out lesson plans for class time. All businesses and industries use their own jargons. Learning this jargon is part of communicating in that particular workplace.

Writing clearly and using correct business form are important on the job. Accurately delivering a message is vital. Employers value workers with the ability to listen to instructions, read instructions, and follow instructions. An employee who can communicate well will be more quickly promoted.

The ability to interpret nonverbal communication of co-workers and customers also makes an employee valuable. However, the smart worker also realizes that certain types of body language are unacceptable in the business world. For example, shaking a finger in another person's face or throwing a chair across the room aren't acceptable.

	Check It Out	**1-5**

All types of work require the ability to communicate. Not all jobs require the same communication skills. Read each of the job descriptions in this exercise. Check the communication skills you think each worker will need in their workplace. You may check several skills.

Workplace No. 1: Jeremy works in a flower shop. He takes orders from customers in the shop and over the telephone. He gets directions for deliveries of orders. He keeps a list of flowers and other materials that must be ordered to make various flower arrangements.

Check the skills that Jeremy uses in his workplace:

_____ Uses proper English	_____ Uses appropriate body language
_____ Writes legibly	_____ Listens to others
_____ Speaks clearly	_____ Uses the telephone properly
_____ Expresses ideas clearly	_____ Takes accurate messages
_____ Understands nonverbal communication	_____ Listens to instructions

Workplace No. 2: A receptionist in a dental office, Sherri greets patients as they come for appointments. She schedules appointments. Each day, she calls patients to remind them of their appointments.

Check the skills Sherri uses in her workplace:

_____ Uses proper English	_____ Uses appropriate body language
_____ Writes legibly	_____ Listens to others
_____ Speaks clearly	_____ Uses the telephone properly
_____ Expresses ideas clearly	_____ Takes accurate messages
_____ Understands nonverbal communication	_____ Listens to instructions

Workplace No. 3: Chef Alex works at the Old Mansion Inn. He prepares each evening's menu, supervises the kitchen staff, and fills the orders that the wait staff brings to the kitchen. He orders the food needed to prepare these meals.

Check the skills that Chef Alex needs in his workplace:

_____ Uses proper English	_____ Uses appropriate body language
_____ Writes legibly	_____ Listens to others
_____ Speaks clearly	_____ Uses the telephone properly
_____ Expresses ideas clearly	_____ Takes accurate messages
_____ Understands nonverbal communication	_____ Listens to instructions

(continues)

(continued)

Workplace No. 4: Hal, an auto mechanic, works in the repair shop of a local car dealership. He checks out and repairs the cars that customers bring into the shop.

Check the skills that Hal uses in his workplace:

_____ Uses proper English	_____ Uses appropriate body language
_____ Writes legibly	_____ Listens to others
_____ Speaks clearly	_____ Uses the telephone properly
_____ Expresses ideas clearly	_____ Takes accurate messages
_____ Understands nonverbal communication	_____ Listens to instructions

Check Your Vocabulary

Read the vocabulary list. These words appear in this chapter. Read the following definitions and place the letter of the correct word on the line in front of the definition.

A	communication	H	listening
B	speaker	I	technological communication
C	listener	J	interpret
D	communication skills	K	reading
E	nonverbal communication	L	slang
F	verbal communication	M	secret language
G	written communication	N	e-mail
		O	colloquialisms

1. _____ Includes writing, reading, listening, and speaking.

2. _____ Communicating using printed words.

3. _____ The sharing of thoughts and ideas among people.

4. _____ Communicating using machines such as the telephone and computer.

5. _____ Words given new meanings rather than their standard English meaning; often used among friends.

6. _____ Sending and receiving messages using spoken words.

7. _____ Possibly the most neglected communication skill.

8. _____ The message sender: the person sharing his ideas and thoughts.

9. _____ Sending messages without using spoken words.

10. _____ Understanding what a speaker's words or gestures mean.

11. _____ Understanding printed or written material.

© JIST Works, Indianapolis, IN

12. _____ The receiver; the person interpreting another person's message.

13. _____ A special interpretation of a word or phrase shared within a certain group.

14. _____ Words that have a certain meaning in a particular region of a country.

15. _____ Electronic mail.

Summing It Up

Communication takes place when one person interprets a message sent by another person. At least two people must be involved for communication to take place. One person must be receiving or listening to the message. Another person must be sending the message. This message may be verbal or nonverbal; nonverbal communication includes gestures and written messages. Misunderstanding and confusion may result when the speaker and the listener aren't communicating the same message.

Communication is a learned activity influenced by family and friends as well as school and life experiences. Poor communication skills can be improved with practice and hard work. With better communication skills, your ability to get and keep a job will improve.

CHAPTER 2

Effective Listening Skills

Have you ever had the feeling, when talking to someone, that the person heard you, but was not really listening? For instance, you come home with the news that you've just been laid off, and your wife or husband says, "That's nice, dear." Communication has taken place, but not effective communication.

Listening skills are important. Listening involves more than simply hearing what is being said.

What Is Listening?

Read aloud John and Millie's conversation. One participant should read John's part, and another should read Millie's part.

John and Millie spend every Tuesday evening bowling in a mixed doubles league. Tonight, to celebrate their smashing success at the lanes, they stop off at the local coffee shop for some refreshments and conversation.

Millie: I am taking a class at technical school next semester. I'm really a little nervous about getting all the work completed for it.

John: I nearly had an accident on the way to the bowling alley tonight. This car just came out of nowhere, and I...

Millie: I wanted to take this class last semester, but I didn't get registered in time. I don't plan to make that mistake again.

John: My insurance rates would have really gone up if I had been in another accident. It wouldn't have been my fault.

Millie: I don't know. If I do well in this class, I just may get my associate's degree.

John: Well, no dents in the car this time. I just hit those brakes like a NASCAR driver. I have great reflexes.

Listening and hearing aren't the same thing. Millie and John could both physically hear the other person. Their ears took in the sound waves produced by the other's voice. Hearing took place, but did anyone listen? Listening involves the mind processing the words being spoken. Millie and John sent messages, but no one received those messages.

| | **Check It Out** | **2-1** |

What's your Listening I.Q.? Answer each of the following questions by checking "Yes" or "No." Be honest with yourself.

	Yes	**No**
1. Do you ever have ear problems that prevent you from hearing clearly?	_____	_____
2. Do you ever finish a friend's sentence?	_____	_____
3. Do you ever daydream because you are sleepy, tired, or hungry?	_____	_____
4. Do you concentrate so much when you take notes that you don't hear the instructor's main points?	_____	_____
5. Have you ever failed to complete work assignments because you didn't follow the directions correctly?	_____	_____
6. Do you understand messages that a speaker sends with his hands and face?	_____	_____
7. Can you listen to a speaker's voice and identify an expression of certain emotions, such as happiness, sadness, anger, or humor?	_____	_____
8. Can you accurately give the details of a telephone message to a friend?	_____	_____
9. Can you repeat and follow the directions to a friend's home?	_____	_____
10. Can you correctly retell a joke or story you have heard?	_____	_____

Look at questions 1–5; give yourself one point every time you answered "No" to one of these questions. Look at questions 6–10; give yourself one point every time you answered "Yes" to one of these questions. Add all the points together. Your instructor will tell you how your Listening I.Q. rates.

Listening Begins with Hearing

Hearing is the first step in the listening process. It is a physical activity. When someone speaks, you hear the voice. Your ears pick up the sound waves produced by the voice. Hearing is an involuntary act. Your ears simply do it. You do not consciously choose to hear.

Hearing can be impaired, as the following story points out.

A prosecuting attorney was questioning a prospective juror for a trial. The lawyer asked the man various questions. Each time, the man asked the lawyer to repeat the question before he would answer it. Finally, the attorney asked the question, "Mr. Knight, do you have difficulty hearing?" After asking to have the question repeated, Mr. Knight said, "No, sir. I'm an excellent driver; I can steer just fine." Mr. Knight was dismissed from serving on the jury because of his hearing impairment.

Like Mr. Knight, people often deny the fact that they can't hear clearly. If you believe that you have a hearing problem, you should seek medical advice. If you ignore the matter, a mild hearing problem could become a serious hearing loss.

And the problem may have a simple solution. People with hearing impairments often use hearing aids or read lips to help them overcome this handicap.

Listening Is a Choice

While hearing is involuntary, listening is a choice. You may hear a voice and choose to ignore it. In this case, no response is made, and the listening process stops. Often we choose to listen if we have an interest in what the speaker is saying.

Listening not only involves the ears, but the mind as well. Your mind must process the words you hear. At times, your mind may choose to block out messages your ears receive; at other times, your brain receives and interprets messages.

If you choose to listen, the listening process continues. The second step of listening is interpreting the speaker's message. To do this, a good listener uses not only the ears but the eyes as well. Certain facial expressions and body movements can help a listener understand the message. A listener's life experiences and attitudes may affect the way she interprets the speaker's words. For this reason, two listeners may listen to the same speaker and have different interpretations of what the speaker says.

These hints can help you listen to learn:

● As the person speaks to you, listen carefully to what he says at the beginning and at the end. Often when someone gives directions or lectures, he states the most important idea at the beginning and then repeats that idea at the end of the talk.

● Listen for important details as the speaker talks. Clue words will help you recognize these details. Examples of clue words are "This is really important," "Remember this," "Point number two is...," or "This will be on the test."

● To help you remember these important points, write them down, so you can review the important points later. Writing will also help your mind focus on these facts.

Check It Out **2-2**

Read the following conversations. Decide if passive or active listening is taking place and explain why you think so.

Conversation No. 1: Jolene and Rochelle both work at a 24-hour restaurant.

Jolene: This new manager doesn't know anything about running this store. Last night, she let the 7-11 shift leave before I even got here. When I got to work at 11, none of the cleaning had been done. The grill hadn't even been cleaned. If this continues, I'm getting a new job.

Rochelle: I guess you'll have to make that decision.

1. Is Rochelle a passive or an active listener? _____

2. Why? _____

Conversation No. 2: Ms. Cornell is the personnel administrator at University Hospital. Henry is applying for a job in the laboratory.

Ms. Cornell: Please fill out this application. Be sure to print clearly. I will check on you in about 10 minutes to see how you're doing and ask you some questions about yourself.

Henry: Thank you, Ms. Cornell. Would you like me to use a pen or pencil when filling out the application?

1. Is Henry a passive or an active listener? _____

2. Why? _____

(continues)

Conversation No. 3: Mr. Sargent teaches at Peabody High School. Lamont and Carmen, students in his English class, are seated at the back of the classroom.

Mr. Sargent: Now class, next Thursday you will be taking an exam. It will cover chapters 23 and 24 on grammar and punctuation. It is important that you go over the exercises about using the comma. Many of you had trouble with the comma when we were doing those exercises.

Carmen: Are you going to the basketball game tonight? I need a ride.

Lamont: I could take you if my brother hadn't already asked his friend.

1. Are Carmen and Lamont passive or active listeners? _____

2. Why? _____

Conversation No. 4: Tina has just returned to the house after a shopping trip. Her brother Anthony is spending the evening watching TV and munching popcorn.

Tina: I just had the most horrible experience. The clerk at the department store thought I was shoplifting. She called the mall security guard before she even let me explain.

Anthony: Hey, Sis! Calm down. Go over that again. Wait a minute; let me turn the TV off first.

1. Is Anthony a passive or an active listener? _____

2. Why? _____

Listening to Directions

Directions guide a listener to a goal. Perhaps the goal is to get to a particular place. Key words aid the listener in following the directions.

Key words given to help a listener find a place fall into three categories:

1. Directional words show the way to a given point.

2. Distance words indicate a measured area or space.

3. Landmarks point out a particular place.

The following chart shows examples of these key words.

Directional Words	Distance Words	Landmarks
Turn right	Go through three doors	At the red barn
Go straight	Two blocks from the stoplight	Beside the courthouse
Follow the curve	Five miles from the intersection	By the house on the hill

Check It Out 2-3

Write a set of directions describing a fire escape route from your classroom to a safe place outside. List the directions step by step.

Step 1: _____

Step 2: _____

Step 3: _____

Step 4: _____

Step 5: _____

Step 6: _____

Underline the key words used in your directions.

Following Instructions

Speakers sometimes give instructions to help a listener complete a task or make something. You must listen carefully to each step in the instructions. By following the instructions one step at a time and in the order given, you can complete a complicated job with ease.

The key words used in instructions include directional words and sequence words. Sequence words give an order to complete the task.

Look at the following chart for some examples.

Sequence Words	Directional Words
First step	Top of the page
Next	Bottom left corner
Last of all	Turn the dial to the left
Second	Center of the page
Number one	Push the red button

To understand instructions, you must concentrate on the words being spoken. Look at the speaker as you listen. Notice any words that he or she stresses. This means that he may slow down his rate of talking as well as being more precise. Watch for anything the speaker writes down. If you have problems remembering instructions, write down the important points.

Check It Out 2-4

Write a step-by-step instructional guide telling how to brush your teeth.

Step 1: _____

Step 2: _____

Step 3: _____

Step 4: _____

Step 5: _____

Look at the instructions you wrote. Underline the key words you used.

Listening to Evaluate

Many times in your life, you must judge what a speaker is communicating to you. A speaker may have a strong opinion about a certain topic and try to convince you to support a cause. It is important that you be able to listen and evaluate what the speaker is saying. This involves more than just hearing his words.

The Sound of a Voice

A monotone voice is flat and unchanging. No emotion is heard as the speaker talks. A monotone voice indicates that the speaker is bored and uninterested. The pitch of a voice is how high or low the words sound. If the speaker's voice rises in pitch, he may be excited about the topic. A lower pitch indicates calmness. The tone of the voice can also suggest the speaker's opinion. As the speaker changes the pitch of her voice and stresses words, her feelings are expressed. Listen for emotions such as anger, sadness, or happiness. A firm voice indicates that the speaker understands the topic. A weak voice may mean that he is unsure of himself or uncomfortable with the subject.

Listen to words that are stressed. When stressing a particular word, the speaker may talk slower and more precisely. He may speak in a louder voice. Notice pauses between words or sentences. A speaker may use a pause to draw a listener's attention to that part of the speech.

Body Action

The politician wants your vote. The salesperson wants your purchase. The animal rights activist wants you involved in his cause. You must listen and judge each speaker's message. You must make the decision after you have evaluated not only what is being communicated, but also how and why it's being communicated.

Watch the hand and body gestures of the speaker. Pounding the desk or pointing shows strong emotions. As the speaker moves closer to an audience, he gets more attention and probably is attempting to make an important point. By remaining behind a lectern or desk, a speaker silently says, "I am the person in charge here." Watch the speaker's facial expressions. A smile, a frown, or a scowl reflects emotion.

Compare Before You Decide

Before you make a decision to buy, vote, or join a cause, know something about the subject or the product. Don't just accept what the speaker tells you. Compare your information to the claims the speaker makes. Make a list of why the speaker is trying to influence you. Finally, list your reasons for buying the product or supporting the speaker. Then make your decision.

Check It Out   2-5

Listen to a radio commercial. Answer the following questions about the commercial.

1. What does the speaker want you to do? _____

   _____

2. Why does the speaker say you should do this? _____

   _____

3. What does the speaker claim about the product or cause? _____

   _____

4. Do you agree or disagree with the speaker? Why? _____

   _____

Watch and listen to a television commercial. Answer the following questions about the commercial.

1. What does the speaker want you to do? _____

   _____

2. Why does the speaker say you should do this? _____

   _____

3. What nonverbal communication does the speaker use in the commercial?

   _____

4. What does the speaker claim about the product or cause? _____

   _____

5. Do you agree or disagree with the speaker? Why? _____

   _____

Check Your Vocabulary

Read the vocabulary list. These words appear in this chapter. Read the following definitions, and place the letter of the correct word on the line in front of the definition.

A hearing
B listening
C hearing impairment
D passive listening
E active listening
F key words

G evaluate
H sequence words
I directional words
J landmarks
K distance words

1. _____ A physical condition that limits a person's ability to hear sounds.

2. _____ Listening in which the listener responds by concentrating on the speaker's words. The listener may ask questions of the speaker.

3. _____ To judge and examine.

4. _____ Words used to show directions, for example, the left side, west, the bottom line.

5. _____ The physical ability to perceive sound.

6. _____ Words indicating a particular place, for example, the red house on the curve, by the large boulder.

7. _____ Listening with little or no response to the speaker.

8. _____ Words that give the listener clues about what the speaker considers important.

9. _____ The act of hearing a speaker and interpreting what the speaker means.

10. _____ Words used to show an order, for example, the second step, point number three, next, following.

11. _____ Words used to show a measured area or space, for example, 3 miles, 5 inches, 70 yards.

Summing It Up

Being a skilled listener is valuable in every part of your life. Listening includes being able to physically hear and mentally process the information gathered through hearing.

The passive listener processes the information but shows little or no response to it. The active listener processes the information and responds by questioning and evaluating the speaker's opinions.

Listening to follow directions and instructions requires an awareness of key words. These words include distance words, directional words, words involving landmarks, and sequence words.

Often, a listener must evaluate what the speaker is communicating. The listener must observe the speaker's words, gestures, and emotions. Gathering information about the topic to form an opinion also helps the listener's understanding.

To improve your listening habits, follow these simple steps:

- **First, act like a listener.** Choose to listen. Stop talking and focus on the speaker. Look at the speaker.

  Concentrate on the words being spoken. Avoid distractions. Don't think about what you are going to say. Just listen.

- **Next, try to interpret what the speaker is saying.** Listen to the words and look for the nonverbal communication going on. Remember listening uses the ears, the eyes, and the mind. Get the whole picture.

- **Now, evaluate what is being said.** You may need to ask a question or ask that something be repeated if you did not understand.

- **Finally, respond to the speaker.** You may just nod to let the speaker know you understand what has been said. Your response may be to say something to the speaker or an action, such as agreeing or disagreeing to do something for the speaker.

Both the social and work worlds highly value the skill of listening. You cherish listening friends because they care enough to accept you and your problems. Listening employees are valued because they can follow instructions and think before they act. With practice, you can be a better listener.

CHAPTER 3

Oral Communication

Oral communication consists of messages sent from one person to another through the spoken word. Examples of oral communication include talking with friends, discussing assignments with co-workers or classmates, instructing someone in how to build a birdhouse, or speaking before a group.

Speaking spreads ideas by using words. Using correct words in speaking is important for two reasons. First, you and your audience must share an understanding of the words that you use. When the speaker and the listener have different meanings for, or definitions of, a word, confusing messages will be sent. Second, the English language has a structure that is considered the correct form of speaking; this is called English grammar. People who use incorrect grammar are often ignored because their speech makes them appear uneducated. If you want people to recognize your ideas, you must use correct grammar.

Your Voice Is a Tool

Your voice is the tool you use to speak. Skillful oral communication requires a clear speaking voice. The way your voice sounds influences the listener's opinion of you and your message. A monotone voice, one with no change up or down in pitch or volume, shows no emotion. Monotones are boring and uninteresting. A voice that sounds too high and squeaky is irritating. A whining voice suggests complaining. An extremely low voice may be so difficult to hear that others just ignore what is being said.

Speaking too slowly causes your voice to be uninteresting, and people may simply quit listening. However, if you talk too fast, the words may become jumbled together and hard to understand. With effort and practice, you can learn to speak at an even rate.

Hearing the same phrases over and over irritates the listener. Phrases such as "you know" or "okay" dominate some people's speech habits or patterns. Eventually, the listener becomes so conscious of the phrase being repeated that the other words aren't even heard. Equally annoying are unconscious habits such as coughing, constantly clearing the throat, or not looking at the listener. Again, with effort and practice, these unconscious and irritating habits can be broken.

Speak Clearly

Articulation refers to the clearness of your speech. Your jaw, tongue, and lips all help you speak plainly. Unclear speech is often the result of laziness of the tongue and lips or just not opening the mouth wide enough.

When words aren't pronounced carefully, mumbling develops. When mumbling, a person lowers his voice and fails to open his mouth. The listener cannot understand the speaker. To correct mumbling, you must open your mouth to speak distinctly and think of each word separately. This takes conscious and consistent effort, but the results are worthwhile.

Sometimes, damage to the mouth causes a person to speak unclearly. A doctor may need to correct this damage. You also use your teeth in speaking, and dental problems can cause your speech to be unclear. You may need to talk to an orthodontist.

A person who is unable to speak clearly may find help through a speech therapist. A speech therapist is qualified to detect particular sounds that are difficult for a person to make. The therapist then uses exercises to improve the clarity of these individual sounds. As the person becomes more conscious of the problem sounds, he can correct those sounds in daily conversations. Through practice, speech therapy may be used to correct old speech habits and develop new ones.

Check It Out 3-1

Fill in the sentence blanks using the word bank below. Do not use any word twice.

oral communication	definitions
grammar	speech pattern
speech therapist	articulation
mumbling	whining
tongue	monotone
habits	low voice
tool	jumbled

1. Lowering your voice and failing to open your mouth when speaking will result in
   _____.

2. Repeating the same phrases, such as "you know" or "okay," can become a part of
   your _____.

3. You use your jaw, _____, and lips in pronouncing words clearly.

4. A _____ voice doesn't change in pitch or volume and is boring.

5. A _____ _____ may analyze an individual's speech difficulties
   and use exercises to improve speech habits.

6. Sending messages from one person to another using the spoken word is called
   _____ _____.

7. An extremely _____ _____ may be difficult to hear.

8. Your voice is the _____ used in speaking.

9. Unconscious _____, such as coughing or clearing the throat when speaking,
   can be irritating to the listener.

10. You need to know the _____ of the words you use when speaking.

11. Speaking too fast causes words to be _____ together and hard to understand.

12. People who use incorrect _____ appear uneducated.

13. The clearness of your speech is called _____.

14. A _____ voice makes the speaker seem to be a complainer.

Good Grammar Counts

Use of proper grammar in conversation reflects a confident, educated person. With practice, using the correct word becomes a habit. The incorrect word just doesn't "sound right" any more.

Check It Out   3-2

Use the following exercise to check your grammar. Circle the correct italic word to complete each sentence.

1. *(Let Leave)* Arnold have the chair.

2. We *(ain't aren't)* going to the party.

3. Maribelle *(sing sings)* country Western music.

4. Mr. and Mrs. Peterson *(was were)* married in 1940.

5. You *(can may)* go to the baseball game.

6. The divers have *(swam swum)* to the ship.

7. Danny *(eat ate)* a whole pizza.

8. The choir *(sing sings)* only classical music.

9. The pitcher *(threw thrown)* a curve ball.

10. Rory *(say said)*, "Meet me at noon."

11. Will you *(sit set)* the box here?

12. Waldo doesn't have *(any no)* pencils.

13. *(Teach Learn)* the part of Emily for the play.

14. The class has *(wrote written)* essays about war.

15. Yesterday, the girls *(lie lay)* in the sun for hours.

16. I *(don't doesn't)* want a copy of that book.

17. The pond has *(froze frozen)* over.

18. The cars *(was were)* caught in a traffic jam.

19. *(Bring Take)* that basket to me.

20. The Nelsons have *(came come)* for a visit.

How did you score? If your score indicates a need for additional help, many resources are available to you. You must be willing to ask for assistance with grammar. Are you a student in a classroom? Ask your teacher or counselor for additional sources of instruction. They may have access to workbooks or textbooks that could help you. Many workbooks offer an individualized program.

Are you out of school? Talk to your local librarian. Many libraries have adult education booklets that are easy to read and that cover basic grammar skills. In some libraries, tutors may also be available through a literacy program. The library also provides an excellent place to study. Be sure to check it out.

Some libraries, schools, and colleges offer computerized programs to aid students in becoming more skilled in the use of grammar. This individualized learning allows you to work at your own speed. Many computerized programs are set up to give you the correct answer if you make a mistake. Computerized learning is fun.

You might know someone who practices good grammar. Just talking to this person on a regular basis will help you improve your oral grammar. Learning to use the correct forms of words on paper is an important first step, but you also need to practice speaking correctly. As you use proper grammar, you will become more skilled in this area. Your ear will become more sensitive to the incorrect use of words.

A clear speaking voice and the use of proper grammar will add to your conversational abilities. If you lack confidence in conversations, you can become a better speaker with practice. As your speech improves, your feelings of confidence will grow. You will be more at ease in conversations.

Starting a Conversation

Learning how to start a conversation will help you in awkward situations. Remember that everyone feels uncomfortable in conversations from time to time. Practice will help you feel more comfortable as you converse with others.

Starting a conversation becomes easier when you focus attention on the other person. If you concentrate on the other person, you will begin to forget about your own feelings. Most people enjoy being made to feel special. They will respond to your attention in a positive way.

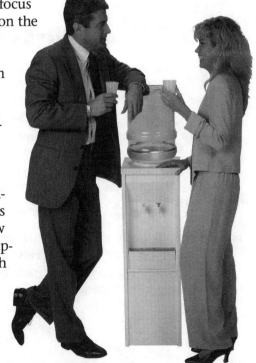

You can focus attention on another person by asking them questions. You need to be careful what type of question you ask. Avoid asking extremely personal questions; they are not appropriate for a new acquaintance or for anyone who might be uncomfortable with certain topics. Questions such as "How much do you make working here?" or "How much did you pay for those new shoes?" are not appropriate. Some people would be offended by such questions.

Avoid asking questions about controversial topics. Questions such as "How do you feel about the new supervisor?" or "What do you think about Mindy's new boyfriend?" could cause embarrassment. Because political and religious beliefs often bring out strongly felt emotions in people, you should avoid these topics when starting a conversation.

Questions involving the situation in which you have met the person would be appropriate. For example, Howie has met Karla while standing in the receiving line at a wedding. He started a conversation like this:

Howie: Are you a friend of the bride or the bridegroom?

Karla: The bridegroom.

Howie: I'm a friend of the bride. Actually, I've known Sheila all my life. She and I were neighbors as children. How do you know James? Have you known him for a long time?

Karla: We work in the same office downtown. I've known him for about three years now. I just met Sheila about three months ago.

Howie: Sheila said that James really enjoys the insurance business. What are your duties in the office?

Karla: I'm the office manager. What type of work do you do?

Notice that as the conversation continues, Karla begins to ask conversational questions also. This helps the conversation continue to develop.

Closed and Open-Ended Questions

Questions can be stated in two different forms: closed questions and open-ended questions. Closed questions may be answered with just one or two words. Look at the conversation between Howie and Karla. What closed question did Howie ask? Some other examples of closed questions include "What type car do you drive?" or "Did you grow up in this town?" or "Are you going to the concert tonight?"

Since the closed question can be answered with only one or two words, the conversation will stop until another question is asked. A closed question gives information, but it doesn't stimulate conversation.

The open-ended question allows the person being questioned to share his opinion. What open-ended questions did Howie ask? An example of an open-ended question is "I see you are driving a Dodge Viper. What do you like about it?" An open-ended question encourages the listener to become a part of the conversation.

If you ask an open-ended question, don't make it too complicated or technical—for example, "I see you are driving a Dodge Viper. What are the latest statistics on its fuel economy and safety record?" The listener may not be able to answer the question unless he is a mechanic. This could cause embarrassment and an awkward situation.

An open-ended question shouldn't influence the listener's answer. For example, "I see you are driving a Dodge Viper. Best little car on the road! How do you like it?" The listener must either agree or disagree with the speaker. Once again, the listener could feel awkward in this situation.

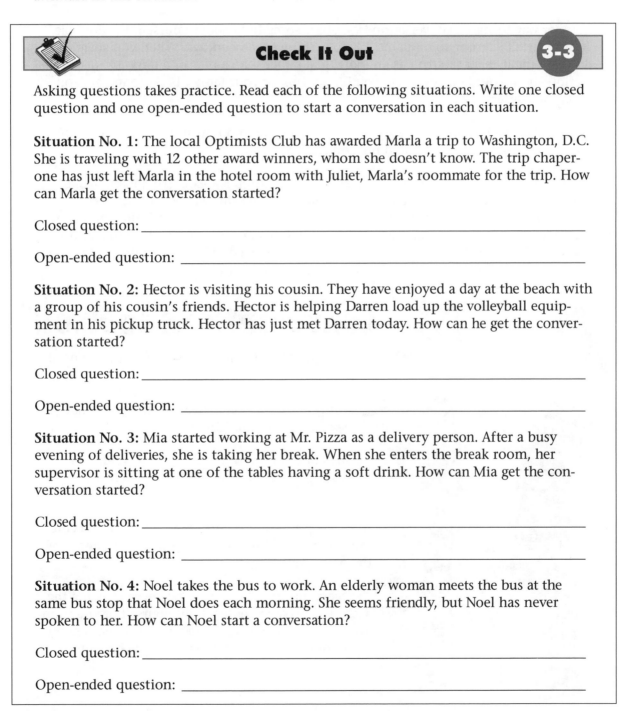

Check It Out   3-3

Asking questions takes practice. Read each of the following situations. Write one closed question and one open-ended question to start a conversation in each situation.

Situation No. 1: The local Optimists Club has awarded Marla a trip to Washington, D.C. She is traveling with 12 other award winners, whom she doesn't know. The trip chaperone has just left Marla in the hotel room with Juliet, Marla's roommate for the trip. How can Marla get the conversation started?

Closed question: _____

Open-ended question: _____

Situation No. 2: Hector is visiting his cousin. They have enjoyed a day at the beach with a group of his cousin's friends. Hector is helping Darren load up the volleyball equipment in his pickup truck. Hector has just met Darren today. How can he get the conversation started?

Closed question: _____

Open-ended question: _____

Situation No. 3: Mia started working at Mr. Pizza as a delivery person. After a busy evening of deliveries, she is taking her break. When she enters the break room, her supervisor is sitting at one of the tables having a soft drink. How can Mia get the conversation started?

Closed question: _____

Open-ended question: _____

Situation No. 4: Noel takes the bus to work. An elderly woman meets the bus at the same bus stop that Noel does each morning. She seems friendly, but Noel has never spoken to her. How can Noel start a conversation?

Closed question: _____

Open-ended question: _____

More Conversation Starters

You can start a conversation by offering a sincere compliment. For example, "You really have a terrific slam-dunk. Where did you learn to play basketball?" Once again, you have focused on the listener. As he responds to the compliment, he will feel more at ease with you.

Be sure that you really mean what you say. People know when someone is being insincere. A false compliment won't be received well.

Another way to start a conversation is to share something about yourself. For example, "I just started learning to oil paint. It's something I really enjoy." When you share in this way, the listener sees you as an individual rather than a part of a large group. Information about your hobbies, a trip you have taken, or your family background are conversation starters.

Be sure that the information being shared doesn't sound boastful. Be sure that it is information you want to share, and not something private.

Discussing a shared interest can also start a conversation. For example, Jonathon and Nate have just met at the annual dinner meeting of the Bird Watchers of America. Jonathon might start the conversation by saying, "I recently returned from a bird counting expedition in Yellowstone National Park. Have you ever been involved in a bird count?" Obviously, Jonathon knows that Nate is interested in birds because they are both at the meeting. Birds are a safe subject to get the conversation started.

Conversations to Avoid

Some types of conversations can cause problems in relationships. Gossip—especially malicious gossip that could damage someone's reputation—can bring a lot of trouble into any group. Do not spread rumors and gossip.

Constant criticism of others threatens relationships. People begin to wonder what the critic is saying about them.

Some people have difficulty telling the truth. Lying can become a habit, and the liar may be unaware of the problem.

Exaggeration isn't lying; it is, however, twisting the facts. Excessive bragging about yourself or your family can cause people to avoid you. They may choose to ignore you rather than listen to the bragging.

In the past, people avoided the topics of politics, religion, and money in polite social conversations because they did not want to oppose others' strong beliefs in these areas. Generally, you should talk about safer subjects unless you are well acquainted with the people joining your conversation.

Bigoted and vulgar conversations insult many people. Using offensive terms in referring to races, ethnic groups, or sexual groups can cause problems in both work and social situations. Constant swearing or the use of vulgar language is socially unacceptable. Using such language is unwise if you want to communicate successfully.

Organizing Conversation Topics

Most conversations don't appear to be organized. Certainly, you didn't plan what you would discuss with your best friend on the way to the shopping mall last weekend. But to make your conversation more effective, you need to think before you speak. If you know you are going to be around someone you want to know better, you may want to think about conversation topics.

Check It Out 3-4

Think of someone whom you would like to know better. It may be someone at work, someone at school, or someone famous you would like to meet. Using the following form, list five topics you could use to start a conversation with this person.

Name of person: _____

Conversation Topics

1. _____

2. _____

3. _____

4. _____

5. _____

Organization by Time Sequence

Some conversations are more than casual. They have a particular purpose. Such a conversation needs to be organized for that purpose.

You can organize a conversation by its time sequence. Such a conversation deals with an event that has taken place. The sequence, or order in which the event happened, is the focus of the conversation.

Check It Out **3-5**

Read the following conversation. Circle the sequence words used in Brandon's description of the wedding.

> **Tina:** Did you go to Rod and Thea's wedding? Tell me all about it.
>
> **Brandon:** Well, first, Rod had trouble getting to the church. His car wouldn't start. He got there about 20 minutes before the ceremony. Next, the flower girl wouldn't hold hands with the ring bearer. After a little coaxing, she went down the aisle. When Thea finally walked down the aisle, everyone breathed a sigh of relief. The rest of the wedding was perfect.

Use sequence words to describe the following situation.

You have just witnessed a car accident. Two cars collided at the corner of Cherry and Hickory Streets. One of the cars went through a red light, entered the intersection, and crashed into the other. An emergency vehicle has now arrived, and a police officer asks you to relate the events of the accident.

Write your description of the accident below. Be sure to include what happened, how it happened, when it happened, who was involved, and where it happened. Use sequence words.

_____

_____

_____

_____

_____

The Logical Approach

Another way of organizing a conversation involves the logical approach. This approach might be used when a speaker tries to persuade a listener to do something. The speaker gives the listener reasons for doing what the speaker wants.

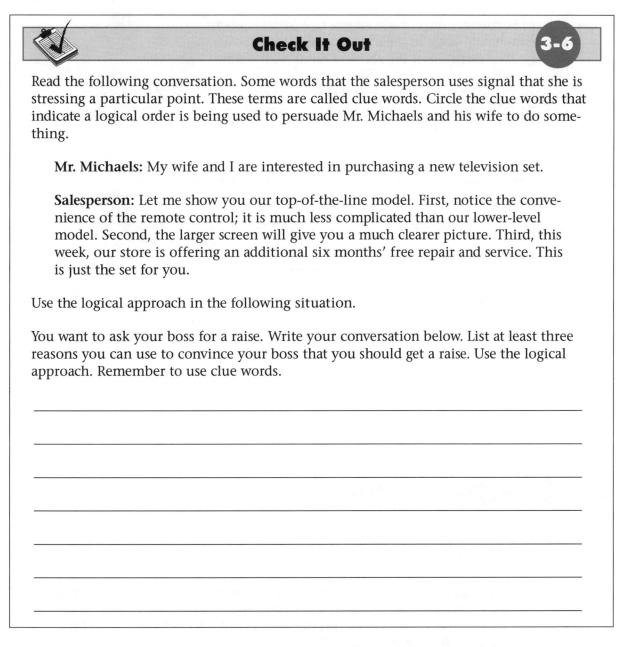

Check It Out
3-6

Read the following conversation. Some words that the salesperson uses signal that she is stressing a particular point. These terms are called clue words. Circle the clue words that indicate a logical order is being used to persuade Mr. Michaels and his wife to do something.

Mr. Michaels: My wife and I are interested in purchasing a new television set.

Salesperson: Let me show you our top-of-the-line model. First, notice the convenience of the remote control; it is much less complicated than our lower-level model. Second, the larger screen will give you a much clearer picture. Third, this week, our store is offering an additional six months' free repair and service. This is just the set for you.

Use the logical approach in the following situation.

You want to ask your boss for a raise. Write your conversation below. List at least three reasons you can use to convince your boss that you should get a raise. Use the logical approach. Remember to use clue words.

_____

_____

_____

_____

_____

_____

The logical approach can also be used to give instructions for doing something. In this case, the speaker gives instructions in a step-by-step pattern. The speaker must view the task in small segments and relate them to the listener in the proper sequence. When the listener completes the final step, the project should be completed.

Effective Communication Skills

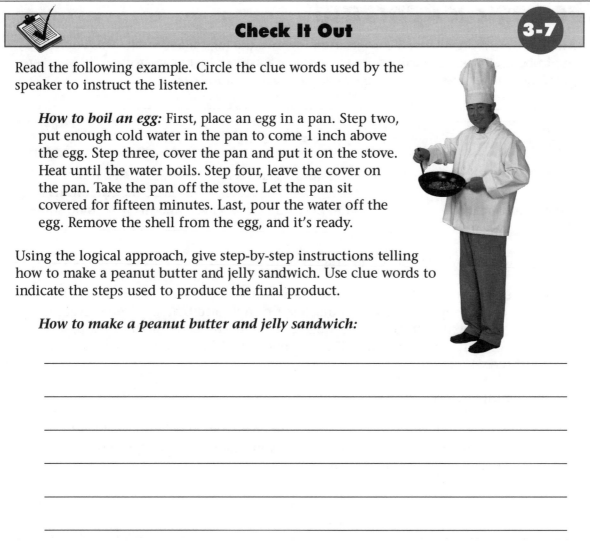

Check It Out 3-7

Read the following example. Circle the clue words used by the speaker to instruct the listener.

How to boil an egg: First, place an egg in a pan. Step two, put enough cold water in the pan to come 1 inch above the egg. Step three, cover the pan and put it on the stove. Heat until the water boils. Step four, leave the cover on the pan. Take the pan off the stove. Let the pan sit covered for fifteen minutes. Last, pour the water off the egg. Remove the shell from the egg, and it's ready.

Using the logical approach, give step-by-step instructions telling how to make a peanut butter and jelly sandwich. Use clue words to indicate the steps used to produce the final product.

How to make a peanut butter and jelly sandwich:

_____

_____

_____

_____

_____

_____

The Assertive Approach

Not all conversations are pleasant. Sometimes, conversations can become arguments when the speaker and the listener disagree. Arguments may result in hurt feelings if words are used without thinking.

Another approach to conversation is the assertive approach. Using this approach, the speaker expresses opinions without hurting someone else. The opinions may not be in agreement with the other person. But when the speaker talks, he talks about the topic and doesn't attack the individual.

The assertive approach allows the speaker to be honest and tactful.

Check It Out

3-8

Read the following example. Circle the compliment used by the speaker to allow her to be kind but firm.

Mom: I know you're watching your cholesterol, Janelle. But scrambled eggs with cheese just this once won't hurt. Have some for breakfast. They're your favorite.

Janelle: Mom, you make the best breakfast in the world. But, if I don't avoid certain foods, I'll never lower my cholesterol level before I go to the doctor next week. I'll just have toast and coffee.

A co-worker has asked you to join the softball league. You don't want to join the league. Below, write a conversation in which you tell your co-worker that you aren't joining the team. Do this in a way that won't hurt your co-worker.

_____

_____

_____

_____

_____

Ending a Conversation

Just as important as getting a conversation started is ending the conversation. Have you ever talked to someone who didn't know how to end a conversation? This person probably repeated the conversation as you listened uncomfortably, wanting to escape.

A good way to end a conversation is to summarize the conversation. For example, "Now, Louis, you were sick and missed two days of work last week. You won't be able to go to the races this weekend because you have to work. Well, maybe next Saturday. Let me know."

Changing positions can also indicate that a conversation is finished. If you are sitting, stand up. If you are behind a desk, walk to the front of the desk. If you are standing and talking, start to turn away from the person. All of these changes are nonverbal ways of saying the conversation is over.

Speaking to Different Audiences

Listeners influence the way you communicate. For example, a chat with a few friends is more informal than a conversation with someone you just met. Situations affect the manner in which you speak to an individual or a group. For example, talking to your co-workers after work is very different than standing in front of them in a business meeting. You can learn how to speak to different audiences.

InTRApersonal Speaking

Do you ever "rehearse" a conversation? As you prepare to ask someone for a favor, do you plan the words you will use in this conversation? This "talking to yourself" is called intrapersonal speech, which literally means "speech inside yourself." Using intrapersonal speech, a person can organize thoughts for future conversations or review a conversation that has already taken place. Sometimes, you may actually speak to yourself aloud. At other times, you may just communicate through thoughts in your own mind, and words may not be spoken. In reality, you are having a conversation with yourself.

This ability to communicate within your own mind is important in organizing your thoughts into a logical form. You will be able to express these thoughts in a clearer way.

InTERpersonal Speaking

Most oral communication takes place as conversation. Every day you express your wants, your emotions, and your ideas through conversation. And others form an opinion of you as they listen to you talk.

As you participate in a conversation, you trade roles with others in the conversation group. At times, you are the speaker, and attention is focused on your words. Sometimes, you are the listener, and your mind processes the words expressed by someone else. Two or more people talking together is called interpersonal speech.

Some conversations feel more comfortable than others do. During a casual conversation with friends or family, the words come easily. Subjects may change as different people express their ideas. Pauses in the conversation take place without anyone feeling a strain. No one expects a continuous flow of words, and no one expects an earth-shattering idea to develop during the conversation.

A conversation with someone in authority, however, or with a stranger, may be more formal and difficult. You may not feel at ease in such a conversation. Pauses in the conversation may seem awkward. You may be so involved in thinking about what you will say next that you fail to listen to the conversation itself. You may be embarrassed if you fail to respond to a question that you are asked during the conversation.

Speaking to a Group

Tall, muscular...a real hunk! On the basketball court, he knew no fear. He could make the tying points with only seconds to play. But, in speech class, the marvel turned into a jellyfish. His fear was so great that he fainted at the podium when he attempted to give his first speech.

For many people, talking to a group is the greatest fear in their lives. Just the thought can cause some people to become ill, lose sleep, or even faint as my basketball friend did. Yet, there are times in our lives when we have to speak to a group. You may be asked to say a few words at a friend's wedding, tell a little about yourself in a work-orientation session, or even make a presentation in a class. So, how can you get comfortable about speaking to a group?

First of all, realize that being a little nervous is normal. Even gifted performers talk about having "butterflies in their stomachs" before going on stage. Nervousness gives you a boost of energy that puts a spark in your speech.

Being prepared will help you overcome some nervousness. Think about what you want to say. If you are actually delivering a speech, you may want to write out the speech and practice it. However, when you give the speech, using just a few notes is usually better than just reading the speech. Notes will help you remember the main topics.

Don't mention your nervousness to the audience. They may not even know that you are nervous. If you mention it, they may focus on that rather than on what you say.

Focusing on your audience will help you forget your own nervousness. Establish eye contact. Don't look at the floor or the ceiling. Don't stare at your notes. Look at the audience members. Chances are, they are on your side. They want to hear what you have to say.

Remember that your body helps deliver your message. Stand tall. Don't slouch. Use hand gestures. Think about where you will hold your hands as you speak.

Keep to the topic. Make your point and move on. At the end of your speech, summarize the main ideas and conclude.

Remember that experience will help you become more relaxed in front of a group. Talking to a group doesn't have to be a miserable experience. It can be enjoyable.

Check Your Vocabulary

Read the vocabulary list. These words appear in this chapter. Read the following definitions, and place the number of the correct word on the line in front of the definition.

A oral communication
B definition
C grammar
D speech therapy
E mumbling
F speech pattern
G intrapersonal speech
H closed question

I open-ended question
J malicious gossip
K exaggeration
L time sequence
M logical approach
N assertive approach
O interpersonal speech

1. _____ Speaking unclearly due to lowering one's voice or speaking without opening one's mouth.

2. _____ The meaning of a particular word or phrase.

3. _____ The act of overstating something; "stretching" the truth.

4. _____ Messages sent from one person to another through speech.

5. _____ A question that allows the person being questioned an opportunity to express his opinion.

6. _____ The order in which something happened; can be used as a way to organize a conversation.

7. _____ The speech habits one has formed.

8. _____ The principles applied in using correct language structure in both speech and writing.

9. _____ Rumors that could damage a person's reputation.

10. _____ The treatment involved in improving one's speaking ability.

11. _____ A question that can be answered using only one or two words.

12. _____ A way of disagreeing in which the speaker expresses an opinion by addressing the topic, rather than attacking the other person.

13. _____ Speaking to one's self, usually in one's mind or by "talking to yourself."

14. _____ A type of conversation in which the speaker gives reasons to convince the listener to do what he wants.

15. _____ A conversation between two or more people.

© JIST Works, Indianapolis, IN

Summing It Up

Oral communication can be a speech, giving instructions, or a chat over the backyard fence. Through the basic form of oral communication—conversation—you express your ideas and wants to those around you. Learning how to start and how to end a conversation are important skills. Most conversations are casual; however, each conversation has some organization.

Conversations with a purpose can be planned in advance. Ways of organizing a conversation include by time sequence, with a logical approach, and with an assertive approach.

A clear speaking voice and the use of proper grammar will add to your conversational abilities. If you lack confidence in conversations, you can become a better speaker with practice. As your speech improves, your feelings of confidence grow. You will be more at ease in conversational situations.

CHAPTER 4

Communicating Over the Telephone

In 1876, Alexander Graham Bell spoke a complete sentence into his new invention, the telephone. His friend on the other end of the line heard the message, "Watson, come here; I want you." That first telephone call went from one room to another.

Today, you can use a telephone to speak to almost anyone on the planet. Cell phone use has become so common that many people are never without a telephone. Now both voices and images can be transmitted through the air. With the right equipment, a professor in New York can teach a class in Denver. He can see the class. The class can see him. Lectures, questions, and answers take place through the airwaves just as if students and teacher were all together in the same classroom.

A part of your life, the telephone is an invaluable aid for maintaining social relationships as well as an essential tool in business. Competent use of the telephone is an important part of developing successful communication skills.

Using the Telephone Properly

Developing correct telephone habits will help you be understood more clearly as you use this machine. Place the receiver in front of your mouth. Direct your voice into the telephone receiver and slow down your rate of speech. Speak distinctly as you talk. As you practice using a clearer telephone voice, it will become a habit. Eventually, you won't be as conscious of your telephone voice.

Remember that the telephone is a machine that transmits sounds. The person you are talking with may also hear any background noises in the room. Be sure to turn off the television or radio when using the phone. With more people using portable phones, it is even more important to be aware of background noises. Eating, drinking, or chewing gum while having a telephone conversation can produce some odd noises. To avoid creating an unpleasant experience for the listener, don't eat, drink, or chew while speaking on the telephone.

Telephone Etiquette

Remember, the person on the other end of the line cannot see you, so be sure to identify yourself at the beginning of the conversation. The end of the conversation must be signaled as well, usually by saying "Good-bye." As you finish a telephone conversation, be sure to place the receiver back on the cradle gently. In this way, you avoid ending the call with a thumping noise in the listener's ear.

Your voice inflection—that is, the tone and pitch of your voice—is more important when you speak on the telephone than in face-to-face conversations. Body language and facial expressions won't have any influence on the listener, who can't see them. A high-pitched, fast-speaking voice may express excitement. A slow, monotone voice may express boredom. Smiling while you speak affects the quality of your voice. The listener will hear a more pleasant voice if you smile as you talk.

Because a telephone conversation happens one-on-one, you need to "tune out" other people in the room while you talk. Avoid trying to have a telephone conversation while talking to someone else in the room. This can confuse the listener on the other end of the telephone conversation.

Check It Out · 4-1

Using the word bank, fill in the blanks to complete the following sentences.

receiver	voice
slower	clearly
end	gently
radio	excitement
smiling	drinking
identify	talk

1. When talking on the telephone, place the _____ in front of your mouth.

2. As you speak on the telephone, direct your _____ into the receiver.

3. You should speak _____ when using the telephone.

4. Speaking at a _____ rate will improve your telephone voice.

5. At the end of the telephone conversation, be sure to place the receiver _____ in the cradle to avoid creating an unpleasant sound in the listener's ear.

6. At the beginning of a conversation, the speakers should _____ themselves.

7. Saying "Good-bye" indicates the _____ of a telephone conversation.

8. _____ while talking on the telephone will make your telephone voice sound more pleasant.

9. Don't _____ to another person in the room while holding a telephone conversation.

10. Avoid eating, _____, or chewing gum while speaking on the telephone.

11. Turn off the television and _____ when using the telephone to avoid interfering background noises.

12. Remember that your voice inflection will express emotions on the telephone. A fast-paced, high-pitched voice could indicate _____ to the listener.

Using the Telephone Directory

Before making a telephone call, you need to know the correct telephone number. The telephone company issues a directory listing the telephone numbers of individual and business customers in its local area. If you don't know a telephone number, this directory is the first place to look. Knowing how to use the telephone directory can save you both time and money.

Telephone directories contain both white pages and yellow pages. When you need information, you may find one of these helpful.

The White Pages

The white pages are divided into three different sections, for residences, businesses, and governmental offices and services.

The residence white pages list the names of most non-business telephone customers in the local area alphabetically (of course, some customers pay for unlisted numbers). The name used is that of the person responsible for paying the telephone bill. The street address and the telephone number appear after the name. The residence white pages are very useful when you know a person's name and need either that individual's telephone number or street address.

The business white pages list alphabetically each local business having a telephone. The business address and telephone number follows the name of the business. No other information is given. The business white pages are helpful if you are calling a particular business or need the address of that business.

The government white pages list a variety of government offices and services. These pages are divided into sections based on the level of government in charge of specific agencies. These sections may include city, town, county, village, township, or state government, as well as schools. In each section, the government offices or schools are listed alphabetically. Both the address and the telephone number appear after the name of the agency or school. The government white pages will assist you in finding the telephone number or address of a particular government office or school.

Usually the white pages are marked to help you easily find the three sections. For example, the government white pages are edged with blue and are called the blue pages. The residence white pages are white. The business white pages are edged with pink.

The Yellow Pages

Many businesses advertise their business services in the yellow pages. For a fee, a business may be listed in the yellow pages. A yellow page listing includes the name of the business, the business address, and the telephone number. Some businesses choose to purchase additional yellow page advertising. In this advertisement, a business can give more information, such as the brands of products that it sells, the services that it offers, or a toll-free number that customers can call.

The yellow pages are organized differently than the white pages. The yellow pages list businesses according to the type of service offered. For example, all travel agencies are listed under the heading "Travel." The service topics are listed alphabetically, and, within each topic, each business is listed alphabetically. So the service "Taxidermy" appears before "Travel," and, under "Travel," "Anderson's Travel Agency" is listed before "Sunny Side Travel." Schools, colleges, hospitals, libraries, government offices, and social service agencies may also be listed in the yellow pages.

To use the yellow pages, you need to know what service you want. For example, if you plan to rent a tent for a camping trip, start by finding "Tents" in the topic listings. You may find a listing such as "Tents-Rental." Since you want to rent, not buy, the tent, check this list. Obviously you don't want a party tent. So you need to look for the businesses renting camping tents. When you have found that type of business, you are ready to call those stores for more information.

The yellow pages can help you find a business service when you don't have a particular store in mind. You may also use the yellow pages to do some at-home shopping. If you want a particular product or service, you can use your telephone to find out who offers the product or service, the cost, and store hours. Larger businesses might even list some of this information in their yellow pages ads. By using your telephone and the yellow pages, you may save time and money, rather than running around looking for what you want.

| | **Check It Out** | 4-2 |

Read each of the following situations. Think about the information needed in each case. In the columns to the right, check the part of the telephone directory that would have this information. Some information may appear in more than one set of directory pages.

Information Wanted	Residence White Pages	Business White Pages	Government White Pages	Yellow Pages
1. An Oriental restaurant in a strange city				
2. A listing of local colleges and universities				
3. The telephone number of James Johnson				
4. The address of Barney's Auto Parts				
5. The address of the county health department				
6. A pizza delivery service in your area				
7. A plumber who is available 24 hours a day				
8. The library branch nearest your home				
9. The telephone number of the downtown auto license office				
10. The telephone number of Joe's Grocery				
11. The telephone number of your barber				
12. The telephone number of Michael Jones of 1214 Main Street				
13. The location of a 24-hour emergency clinic				
14. The telephone number of the Hillside School on Grande Road				
15. A listing of the museums in your city				
16. Public transportation services available				

(continues)

Information Wanted	Residence White Pages	Business White Pages	Government White Pages	Yellow Pages
17. The telephone number of the Jonesville Zoo				
18. The location of a dance studio				
19. The telephone number of the United States Post Office				
20. The telephone number of the Kiddie Care Center on Gray Road				

The Directory's Special Assistance Sections

The telephone directory contains many special assistance sections for customers. These sections can save you time and money as you use the telephone.

Billing, Repair, and Special Services

These pages provide information about how the local telephone company bills you and how you may pay your bill. You may also find information about financial aid programs that lower the bills of those who qualify, and what to do if your bill can't be paid on time. A telephone number is given to call if you have a question about your local bill.

If you use a different company for your long-distance service, you will need to know the name of that company. The telephone directory will have a list of long-distance providers and their telephone numbers. If you have a billing problem, you may use one of these numbers to contact your long-distance provider.

The telephone numbers you need to call for repair service to your telephone or to a telephone line appear in a special section of the directory. Basically, if the repair problem occurs in the telephone line outside your home, the telephone company won't charge for sending a technician. However, if the telephone or the telephone lines inside your home need repair, a service fee may be charged. You may want to determine the location of the problem before calling for this service. For a monthly fee, you can buy a maintenance plan that applies to repairs inside your home.

If you need to have your telephone service started, changed, or moved, the telephone directory lists the telephone number that puts you in contact with someone for these services.

The directory offers instructions on how to place a variety of telephone calls, including local, long-distance, and toll-free. If you have trouble making a call, you may need help from a telephone operator. Using the information in the directory, you can place an operator-assisted call. A service fee is usually charged when an operator helps you make a local or long-distance call.

Emergency Information

The universal emergency telephone number in the United States is 911. Dial this number when you need an immediate response by the fire department, police or sheriff departments, or the ambulance or emergency medical services (EMS). This emergency number may save your life some day.

In the front of the directory, other emergency phone numbers are listed. It is wise to post these emergency numbers near your telephone. As an additional precaution, add your own emergency telephone numbers, such as your doctor, dentist, and a helpful neighbor. In an emergency, you may forget an otherwise familiar telephone number.

Remember that these are **emergency** telephone numbers. If you need to contact the police, the fire department, or the ambulance service for a non-emergency reason, look in the white pages for office numbers to call. Using emergency telephone numbers in non-emergency situations is illegal.

Directory Assistance

Sometimes, a telephone number isn't listed in the directory or the listing is new. In this case, you need to call directory assistance. Look in the directory for the telephone number of the directory assistance operator. This information will be found in the telephone directory under the heading, "Directory Assistance."

When you call directory assistance, the operator will need to know the name of the individual or business you are trying to call. This would be the head of the household or the correct business name. The address may help the operator find the correct number, especially if the last name is common in that area. Using this information, the operator will connect you to a machine that will give you the needed telephone number. Write the number down.

The directory assistance operator should be used only when you cannot find the telephone number in the telephone directory. Many telephone companies will charge you a fee for using the directory assistance service. If you do obtain a number through directory assistance, write the telephone number down to avoid having to pay for another call in the future.

Some individuals do not want their telephone numbers made available through the telephone directory; they have unlisted telephone numbers. The directory assistance operator is not allowed to release unlisted numbers. The only way to get an unlisted telephone number is to ask the person for it.

In the telephone directory, usually on the back cover, a page is provided for your own personal telephone list. You will save time and money in the future if you take a few moments to write out the numbers that you call on a regular basis, as well as directory-assisted numbers.

Check It Out   4-3

Use a telephone directory to find out the following information. Fill in the information needed to answer each question. You may use both the white and yellow pages.

1. What is the emergency number for reaching the fire department?
   _____

2. What is the telephone repair service number? _____

3. The telephone number of Twila's Pet Boutique, a new business in town, isn't listed in the telephone directory. How will you find the number? _____

4. What is the telephone number of the Poison Control Center? _____

5. What is the telephone number of the emergency room of a local hospital?
   _____

6. On your telephone bill, you have a long-distance charge for a call that you didn't make. What should you do? What is the telephone number that you should dial?
   _____

7. Someone has spray painted the sidewalk near your home. You want to report this vandalism to the local police. What telephone number should you dial?
   _____

8. When you check the telephone directory, you cannot find the telephone number of Roman Estes, who recently moved to the city. What do you need to do to get his telephone number? _____

9. What is the telephone number of a supermarket near your home?
   _____

10. What is the telephone number of the local fire department in a non-emergency situation? _____

11. What is the telephone number of the American Red Cross? _____

12. You can't find the telephone number of Gina Lilliano in the telephone directory. You call the directory assistance operator; you are told that it is an unlisted number. How can you contact Gina by telephone? _____

13. You are moving into a new apartment. You want a telephone installed. What telephone number should you call to make the arrangements to have this done?
    _____

14. What is the telephone number of the nearest post office? _____

15. What is the telephone number of the county health department?
    _____

Dialing a Telephone Call

Before making a telephone call, be sure that you have the correct telephone number. Put the telephone receiver to your ear, and listen for the dial tone. This steady, neutral tone tells you that the telephone is functioning and ready to receive your call. (If you don't hear a dial tone, hang up and check it one more time. If you do not hear a dial tone then, the telephone or the telephone line may need repair service.)

After hearing the dial tone, carefully dial the telephone number. You will hear one of two sounds: the ringing of the other telephone or a "busy" signal (a beeping sound). The busy signal tells you that someone is using the telephone that you are trying to call. You need to hang up and try to place the call later.

If the other telephone rings, your call has gone through. Allow the telephone to ring 6 to 8 times before you hang up. If the person you are calling is slow getting to the telephone, you need to allow them enough time. If you call an elderly or disabled person, allow some extra rings. If you call a business, remember that the person answering the telephone may be on another telephone line or involved with another customer.

When someone answers the telephone, identify yourself. Give both your first and last name, and briefly explain the reason for your call. When the telephone call is completed, indicate the end of the conversation before hanging up. To do this, you may summarize the conversation, thank the other person for his time, or simply say "Good-bye."

When you place a telephone call, you may be greeted by a machine-activated message. A receptionist in a business may ask you if you want to leave a message on a person's voice mail. Many businesses and individuals now use voice mail or an answering machine to take messages when no one can answer the telephone.

If you get a machine, listen carefully to the message. You may be asked to remain on the telephone until someone can take your call. If you do not want to wait, you may hang up and call back later. You may be asked to wait for a beep and to leave a message. Leave your name, telephone number, and a brief message telling the reason for your call. Be sure to speak slowly and clearly when you leave your message.

NOTE

After the telephone has rung several times, you may get a message from the telephone company. It will tell you that you may leave a message with the telephone company to be delivered later; however, you will also be told that you will be charged for this. If you do not want to pay to leave a message, just hang up or let the telephone continue to ring. If you use an individual's or business's voice mail or answering machine, you will not be charged.

Check It Out — 4-4

Review the information about placing a telephone call by answering the following questions.

1. Why should you allow the telephone to ring several times before hanging up?
    _____

2. What should you do if you get a busy signal? _____

3. How should you identify yourself when the person answers the telephone? Why is this a good idea? _____

4. What does the dial tone tell you about the telephone? What should you do if you cannot get a dial tone? _____

5. How could you indicate that the telephone conversation is over?
    _____

6. What should you do if you don't know the other person's telephone number?
    _____

7. What information should you leave on an answering machine or voice mail?
    _____

Direct-Dialing a Long-Distance Telephone Call

The least expensive way to place a long-distance telephone call is to dial direct. If you call the operator to place a long-distance call, you will pay more for the call. Use the operator only when you have difficulty in placing a call or when you are making special calls such as a "person-to-person" call or a "collect" call. Directions for placing long-distance calls can be found in the telephone directory under the heading, "Local and Long-Distance Calling."

Different sections of the country have been assigned three-digit numbers called area codes. To make a long-distance telephone call, you need to know the area code of the telephone number that you are calling. If you don't know the area code, you will find an area code map in the telephone directory. Look for the section entitled, "Area Codes and Time Zones Map."

To make a direct-dial, long-distance call within your own area code, you should dial 1 and the telephone number. It is not usually necessary to dial your area code; however, in some places you may need to dial "1" followed by your area code. If the long-distance call is to outside of your area code, dial 1 and the area code followed by the telephone number.

Toll-free numbers allow another type of long-distance call. Many businesses use toll-free numbers to let their customers call at the company's expense. You may want to use a toll-free number to place a catalog order or to file a complaint concerning a new appliance. Toll-free telephone numbers use the following area codes: 800, 877, and 888. To dial a toll-free number, dial 1, then the toll-free area code, and finally the telephone number.

Remember that the area codes 900 and 976 offer information for a charge. If you don't want anyone to use these numbers on your telephone, you can have these numbers blocked on your telephone without a charge to you. The Customer Service department of your telephone provider can do this for you.

Operator-Assisted Telephone Calls

Not all calls can be made without the assistance of an operator. Both person-to-person calls and collect calls need an operator to complete the call.

Person-to-Person Calls

You can place a person-to-person, long-distance telephone call when you are interested in speaking to only one particular person. When the call is placed, the operator will ask to speak to that particular person. If the person is unavailable, the operator will ask you to try calling at another time. You won't be charged for the call unless you actually speak to the person.

To make a person-to-person telephone call within your area code, dial 0 followed by the telephone number. If you want to call outside of your area code, dial 0 and the area code followed by the telephone number. Wait for the operator to come on the line. Tell the operator, "I'm making a person-to-person call." Give the operator the name of the person you are calling.

Collect Calls

You might need to make an operator-assisted collect call if you are using someone else's telephone or don't have enough change when you are using a pay phone. When the call is placed, the operator will ask the person answering the telephone if he will accept the charges for the telephone call. If that person accepts the charge, the operator will tell you that the call can go through. If the charges are not accepted, you won't be able to talk to anyone.

To make a collect call within your area code, dial 0 and the telephone number. If the call is to outside of your area code, dial 0 and the area code followed by the telephone number. Wait for the operator to come on the line. Tell the operator you are placing a collect call and give the operator your name.

Telephone Calling-Card Calls

Many people have a telephone calling-card. This is a credit card for placing long-distance calls. The calling-card has a number, which is used to charge long-distance calls when you aren't calling from your home telephone. Each month, any calling-card telephone call charges appear on your telephone bill.

Depending on your long-distance phone company, this procedure will vary. Here are the basics for placing a calling-card call. To call within your area code, dial 0 and the telephone number. To call outside of your area code, dial 0 and the area code followed by the number. In a short time, you should hear a special tone. This tells you to dial your calling-card number. If you don't hear the tone, wait for the operator to come on the line. You give the operator your calling-card number and the operator connects your call.

Prepaid Calling Cards

Prepaid calling cards may be purchased in discount stores, convenience stores, drug stores, and numerous other places. When you buy a card, you are purchasing a certain number of long-distance telephone minutes. To use the card, you dial the numbers indicated on the card. The directions are usually given in three or four steps.

When the call is finished, the number of minutes used is deducted from the total minutes on the card. If you still have minutes left, you may use the card again and again until the minutes have all been used. While you are talking, you will be warned when you have 2 or 3 minutes left. When those minutes run out, the call disconnects or you may be able to buy more minutes.

Long-Distance Access Numbers

You can also make a long-distance telephone call by using a telephone company's long-distance access number. Each long-distance provider has its own access number and its own long-distance rates. If you want to use this service, you will need to find the company you want to use.

To use an access number, you must dial it first. Then you dial 1, the area code, and the telephone number. You will be billed for the call.

Dialing a Wrong Number

On some occasions, you may dial a telephone number, and a total stranger answers. You suddenly realize that you have dialed a "wrong number." Before hanging up, check the telephone number. Ask, "Is this 544-3210?" If the stranger answers, "No, it is not," you have probably made a mistake when dialing the number. If the stranger says, "Yes, it is," you need to check whether this is the person or business you wanted to talk to. Ask, "Is this the Pizza Patio?" If the stranger says, "No, it isn't," you need to check the telephone number in the telephone directory. You may have copied the telephone number incorrectly. You should politely respond, "I'm sorry. I have dialed the wrong number." If you dial an incorrect long-distance call, dial "0" (operator) to report the mistake. If you don't report this mistake, you will be billed for a telephone call that you dialed in error.

 Check It Out 4-5

Read the information given about each of the telephone calls described below. In the column titled "You Dial," give the telephone number and any other information needed to complete the call. You may need to use a telephone directory to get some of the information needed to complete the telephone calls.

For this exercise, pretend that your name is Lynn Lawrence. You live in Moosehead, Maine. The area code is 207. Your telephone number is 262-8041. Your calling card number is 207-262-8041-2637.

Information Given	You Dial
1. Call Ilena Fields at number 744-3321. The area code is 986.	
2. Call the Whoopee Skydiving Club in Santa Fe, New Mexico, at 610-8213.	
3. Use your calling card. Call the following number: (405) 153-9630.	
4. Call the Lobster Dip Inn to make a reservation. The telephone number is (800) 587-2302.	
5. You call Ed's Coffee Shop at telephone number 606-4488. A woman answers, "Hello, this is the Brown residence." What do you say?	
6. Call the following number: (207) 897-8934. It is a local long-distance call.	
7. Place a collect call to this telephone number: (478) 333-9216.	
8. You want to talk to Hal Hansen at 297-4433. The area code is 756.	
9. Using a long-distance access number 10-10 2020, call 903-5758 in area code 343.	
10. You want all 900 and 976 numbers blocked from your telephone number. What will you do?	

Using a Pager

Pagers are another way of contacting someone when you aren't able to reach them on the telephone. Pagers are useful in the workplace. "On call" workers, such as medical personnel and utility crews, often use pagers in case of emergencies.

Like a telephone, a pager has a pager number. To reach the individual you must know that number. Since there is no directory of pager numbers, you can not look it up. The person you are paging must give you the number.

Use a telephone to dial the pager number. You will hear a dialing sound, but no one will greet you with a friendly "Hello." Instead you may hear a message that tells you to dial your own telephone number. In this case, just follow the instructions. The number you dial will appear on the receiver's pager screen.

Some pagers are connected to voice mail. If you dial the pager number, you will be connected to it, and you may leave a message. Be sure to include your telephone number.

To indicate that a message has been left on the pager, it will "beep" or "vibrate" depending on its setting. Since a pager can't be used to return a call, the message receiver must get to a telephone to contact you.

Receiving a Telephone Call

Knowing how to receive a telephone call is just as important as knowing how to make one. When answering the telephone, speak distinctly and identify yourself. For example, "This is the Johnson residence. Kendra speaking." or "Hello. This is Kendra Johnson."

If you answer a telephone in a business situation, you may be instructed to use a particular greeting common throughout the company. The person answering a business telephone must sound enthusiastic and interested. This person may be the customer's first contact with the company. A customer's opinion will be affected by this contact.

Wrong Number Calls

You may answer the telephone and discover that the caller has dialed the wrong number. If this happens to you, politely tell the person that they have a wrong number. If possible, ask the person to repeat the number they intended to dial. He may discover that he misdialed or perhaps he needs to check the telephone directory for the correct number. By taking the time to do this, you may be able to avoid getting another "wrong number" call from him.

Repeatedly getting "wrong number" calls can become annoying. If you receive repeated calls for the same business or the same person, you may want to consider changing your telephone number. The customer service department of the local telephone company will give you information about how this is done and what the cost for the change might be. Before you decide to change your telephone number, consider the inconvenience. Your friends and acquaintances would need to be informed of your new number because it wouldn't be listed in the current telephone directory.

Machine Calls

You may answer the telephone and discover that you are talking to a machine. Businesses use mechanized calling to inform customers that their catalog order has arrived and may be picked up at the local store. A machine may try to sell you something, or it may ask you to be a part of a survey. In both of these cases, you may be asked to push various buttons on a touch-tone telephone to indicate your answers to questions. You may also be asked to respond verbally. You may choose to "talk" to the machine by following its directions. If you don't want to "talk," hang up the telephone.

Telemarketing

Many companies sell their products through telephone sales, or telemarketing. You may receive a telemarketing call from a real live person. If you wish to listen to the sales information, continue the conversation. If you don't want to listen, simply say, "I'm sorry, I'm not interested." Usually the telemarketer will respond by trying one more time to convince you to buy his product. If you are still not interested, very firmly reply, "I'm not interested." If the caller still persists, hang up.

Before agreeing to purchase something from a telephone salesperson, stop and think. If you are really interested, get the information. Ask the telemarketer to call back in one or two days. Telemarketing sales succeed by forcing the consumer into a spontaneous decision. Without thinking, you may be purchasing something you don't want, don't need, or can't afford. If the company really is legitimate, the salesperson will call back as you requested.

Some charitable organizations use telemarketing to raise funds for various projects they sponsor. This is done in different ways. Sometimes, an organization will hold a phone-a-thon. Volunteers for the organization call people in the community to ask for donations to the organization. All of the money donated to the phone-a-thon goes to the sponsoring organization. Some organizations hire a telemarketing company. In that case, the telemarketing company receives part of the money collected for its work. The remainder goes to the charity.

Whatever the method, you have the right to know how your donation is being used.

In dealing with telemarketing sales or donations, remember this rule: **Never, Ever Provide a Credit Card Number over the Telephone**. *If the telemarketer won't bill you, refuse to make the purchase or the donation.*

Prank Calls

Another type of call that you may receive is a form of harassment. Sometimes when children are left at home alone for a long period of time, they may use the telephone as a toy. Such prank calls are irritating.

Harassing calls are more serious. People who are afraid to talk to another person directly may use the telephone to make threats, use abusive language, or breathe heavily into the phone. The caller tries to frighten his victim. Using the telephone in this way is unlawful. Depending on the state where you live, the laws regulating such acts vary.

What should you do if you receive this type of telephone call? According to the telephone company, the best action is no action. The caller wants to know that you are upset. Don't say anything, even if you think you know the person. Don't act shocked or angry. Don't ask, "Who is this?" Just quietly hang up the receiver. If the phone rings again, don't answer it.

If the harassment continues for a long period of time, you should contact the telephone company in your area for help. Check the telephone directory for the number of the customer service department. The telephone company can offer various ways to stop the harassing calls. These solutions may vary from one location to another. Some of the methods will be free, and some will involve a charge. You, the customer, will make the choice of what method you wish to use.

Taking a Telephone Message

Learning to take a telephone message accurately comes in handy. Socially, getting a telephone message incorrect can mean embarrassment. In the business world, an incorrect telephone message can mean lost customers, lost money, and lost time.

When taking a telephone message, listen carefully. Find out whom the caller wants to contact with the message. Write the message in clear handwriting. If you don't write clearly, you should print the message. After you have written the message, repeat what you have written to the caller. Be sure to place the message where the person receiving the message will see it. As soon as possible, check to be sure that the person saw the message.

When taking the message, record the time of the call. This will help avoid confusion if the two people have contacted each other in the meantime. Get the name of the caller. Be sure you have both the first and last name. Just the first name may not be enough to identify the caller. Ask the caller to spell the name if you aren't sure of the spelling.

Sometimes, the message may just be to return the call. Give the caller an opportunity to leave a more detailed message. Ask if this is an urgent situation.

Get the caller's telephone number. If this is a long-distance call, check to see if the area code is different than the local area code. Repeat the telephone number to the caller.

Sign your name at the end of the message. This will allow the receiver to ask you any questions about the call if there isn't enough information in the message.

 Check It Out 4-6

Read each of the following telephone conversations. Write the message in the form that you would use to deliver the correct message.

Conversation No. 1: 9:30 a.m., Monday, April 4

You: Good morning! Public Library. May I help you?

Caller: May I speak to Mr. Jonathon Phillips?

You: Mr. Phillips isn't in. May I take a message?

Caller: This is Yvonne Garcia. I represent the Windows on the World Book Program. I would like to set up an appointment with Mr. Phillips. My telephone number is 663-5112.

```
☎ TELEPHONE MEMO ☎

To: _____

Time: _____ am/pm Date: _____

Caller: _____

Telephone No. (_____) _____

Message: _____

_____

        Signed:_____
```

(continues)

Conversation No. 2: 11:15 a.m., Tuesday, July 11

You: Good morning! Uptown Hair Stylists. May I help you?

Caller: This is Malcolm Collins. May I speak to Marilee Wendall?

You: Marilee isn't available right now. May I take a message?

Caller: I would like to have Marilee style my hair tomorrow morning. My telephone number is 893-4536.

☎ **TELEPHONE MEMO** ☎

To: _____

Time: _____ am/pm Date: _____

Caller: _____

Telephone No. (_____) _____

Message: _____

_____

Signed:_____

Conversation No. 3: 1:00 p.m., Friday, June 12

You: Good afternoon. Mr. Williams's office. May I help you?

Caller: This is Bob Carter. I won't be able to play golf with Mr. Williams this afternoon. Have him call me at 742-0033. Maybe we can play tomorrow.

☎ **TELEPHONE MEMO** ☎

To: _____

Time: _____ am/pm Date: _____

Caller: _____

Telephone No. (_____) _____

Message: _____

_____

Signed:_____

Conversation No. 4: 2:30 p.m., Thursday, March 12

You: Good afternoon! Washington High School. May I help you?

Caller: May I speak with Ms. Karen Monroe?

You: Ms. Monroe is in class. May I take a message?

Caller: This is Deborah Friar. I would like a parent conference with Ms. Monroe sometime this week. I work from 7 till 3. She may call me at work. The telephone number is 337-8469.

☎ **TELEPHONE MEMO** ☎

To: _____

Time: _____ am/pm Date: _____

Caller: _____

Telephone No. (_____) _____

Message: _____

_____

Signed: _____

Using a Cell Phone

Using a cell phone is a little different than using other telephones. First, it must be "powered up." In other words, the power button is pushed. Wait a few seconds, and a message will appear on the screen saying that the phone is ready for use.

Next, dial the telephone number, which will appear on the phone's screen. Check the number. If it is correct, push the send button. The sound of the other telephone ringing indicates that the call has been placed. Wait for an answer. If no one answers, push end or disconnect.

Perhaps when you check the screen, you discover that you dialed the wrong number. Just press the end button, dial again, and continue with the call.

Telephone directories don't list cell phone numbers, and the directory assistance operator can't give you a cell phone number. You must get this information from individuals. However, you can put frequently used telephone numbers (for both cell and regular phones) in your cell phone directory. Once these numbers are programmed into your cell phone directory, they are available wherever your cell phone goes.

Each cell phone has its own unique features. Some are programmed to recognize their "owners'" voices. If the owner simply says the name of a person in his cell phone directory into the receiver, the number will be dialed. If you dial a telephone number and forget to press "send," a "talking" cell phone will remind you by asking "Who are you calling?"

Cell phone providers have different service areas. It is possible when traveling that you may get out of your company's service area. When this happens, the cell phone "roams." In other words, the cell phone may still be used; however, a second provider is giving you service. When this happens, the word "roaming" will appear on the cell phone screen. If you make a call, the roaming provider's charge will be added to your monthly cell phone bill. The charge will probably be greater than the normal fee because both your provider and the roaming provider will be charging you. Check with your service provider before you travel to find out the areas covered by your service plan.

Cell phones can be unreliable. They can fade out, or voices may be garbled. This may happen when traveling from one service area to another. Mountains and large buildings can cause interference with cell phone reception. Being in a certain part of a building—for instance, a basement—may be a hindrance in making or receiving a cell phone call.

Many companies offer a variety of cell phone plans. The prices and number of minutes provided vary greatly. In many cases, you must agree to use the plan for a certain length of time or pay a penalty. Be sure to check a variety of plans before you sign a contract.

Cell Phone Etiquette

Cell phones can be an annoyance to others when used in thoughtless ways. For example, answering your cell phone while having dinner with a friend makes that person feel that you are more interested in your phone message than in spending time together. So unless it is an emergency situation, turn off the cell phone during your conversation.

In public places, find a private area to use your cell phone. Talk in a way that lets the other caller hear you, but that doesn't disturb those around you.

Think before you talk about something private on your cell phone. A cell phone is not secure. Others may be listening to your conversation.

Using a cell phone requires your attention. For this reason, driving while using a cell phone is dangerous and possibly illegal.

When in public, it is best to turn off your cell phone. The beeper or voice mail may be used to direct your calls. A cell phone should not be used in a house of worship; at a movie, a concert, or a play; or while going through a drive-thru service. You may be asked not to use it at certain times on an airplane flight as it interferes with some radio-based monitoring equipment. You may see signs in other public places asking that cell phones be turned off and not used.

 Check Your Vocabulary

Read the vocabulary list. These words appear in this chapter. Read the following definitions, and place the number of the correct word on the line in front of the definition.

A	receiver	M	direct dialing
B	cell phone	N	911
C	cradle	O	directory assistance
D	telephone directory	P	dial tone
E	white pages	Q	busy signal
F	yellow pages	R	area code
G	voice mail	S	person-to-person call
H	prepaid calling card	T	collect call
I	unlisted telephone number	U	wrong number
J	operator-assisted call	V	toll-free numbers
K	long-distance call	W	telemarketing
L	calling-card call	X	harassing call

1. _____ Three-digit number assigned to a particular geographic location.

2. _____ Dialing a long-distance telephone number without using a telephone operator.

3. _____ A way to leave a message when the caller doesn't answer the telephone.

4. _____ A telephone call charged to a telephone credit card.

5. _____ A wireless telephone that may be used almost anywhere.

6. _____ The telephone number called to find an unknown telephone number.

7. _____ The U.S. universal emergency telephone number.

8. _____ A book compiled by the telephone company listing telephone numbers and other information about using the telephone.

9. _____ A telephone call that requires an operator's help.

10. _____ Steady tone heard when a telephone is removed from the cradle; indicates that the telephone is working properly.

11. _____ 800, 877, and 888.

12. _____ A telephone calling card that is bought before it is used to make long-distance calls.

13. _____ The part of the telephone that transmits sound.

14. _____ The part of the telephone directory listing the names, addresses, and telephone numbers of individual and business customers as well as government offices.

15. _____ A beeping sound heard after dialing; indicates that someone is using the telephone line that was dialed.

16. _____ A long-distance call in which the caller asks the person being called to pay the charge.

17. _____ The part of the telephone directory listing businesses and organizations by the type of service they offer.

18. _____ A telephone call outside your local area, for which an additional toll is charged.

19. _____ A telephone number not listed in the telephone directory at the person's request.

20. _____ A long-distance telephone call placed to a particular person.

21. _____ Dialing an incorrect telephone number.

22. _____ A method many companies use to sell their products over the telephone.

23. _____ A telephone call that is meant to harass or frighten the caller.

24. _____ The part of the telephone that holds the receiver.

Summing It Up

The telephone is an essential tool in our social and work lives. Technology has made the telephone portable, so it can now be used in public as well as private places. Using the telephone properly is valuable both on the job and in your own life. Practicing a few simple rules will help you be successful.

Telephone Rules

- **Speak clearly into the receiver.** Be careful of background noises when using the telephone.

- **Identify yourself.** Listen carefully when the other person speaks.

- **Be considerate of others**, especially when you use a phone in a public place. Try to find a private place to talk.

- **End the conversation properly.** When you have finished your telephone call, indicate that the conversation is over by saying "Good-bye."

The telephone directory is a source of information when using the telephone. Learning how to use the telephone directory will save you time and money. When you need information, look there first.

Developing good telephone skills will help you on the job. Taking telephone messages correctly will prevent embarrassing situations and make you a highly valued employee.

CHAPTER 5

Messages Without Words

While shopping in the mall, you pass a person you have never met before. Do you smile or frown? How does this stranger react? Do your eyes meet, or do you look away? Does the pace of your walking change as you approach each other? As you come closer, do you move to the other side of the walkway or continue on your original path?

This is nonverbal communication. No words are spoken, but you are communicating. By observing and interpreting the stranger's actions, you receive a message. At the same time, the stranger receives a message from you by observing and interpreting your actions.

Check It Out 5-1

As you read the following situations, consider the nonverbal communication being sent.

Situation No. 1: It's 8:45 p.m. The store lights dim, and the manager announces over the intercom that the store is closing in 15 minutes. As several customers line up at her register, Joanne, the checker, groans. She grabs her customer's credit card and passes it through the machine with the force of a prizefighter. She bags the merchandise and tosses the bag into the cart. Then she taps her fingers on the counter as the customer signs the receipt. This customer has just received some nonverbal messages from Joanne.

1. List the nonverbal actions Joanne used to communicate with her customer.

_____

_____

_____

2. What is Joanne's communication telling her customer?

_____

_____

_____

Situation No. 2: On another evening in the store, Joanne is again at the checkout counter. The manager gives the closing announcement. Several customers line up at Joanne's checkout lane. Joanne looks up and smiles at the first customer. She whistles while she rings up the sale. She runs the credit card through the machine and bags the merchandise while the customer signs the receipt. She hands the customer her receipt before greeting the next customer. This customer has also received some nonverbal messages from Joanne.

1. List the nonverbal actions Joanne used to communicate with her customer.

_____

_____

_____

2. What is Joanne's communication telling her customer?

_____

_____

_____

Body Action

One form of nonverbal communication, body action, expresses the messenger's emotions. Slamming a door, pounding on the desk, or kicking the dog are examples of body action. Some body actions that would be harmful or threatening to another person wouldn't be considered acceptable in our society. As a responsible person, you must be in control of your body actions.

Interpreting body actions accurately makes communicating with other people easier. To know what message is being sent, you must view the entire situation. If you don't observe and interpret the body actions correctly, you may get the wrong message.

| ![] | **Check It Out** | **5-2** |

Consider this situation: Glenda walks into the house as the door slams. What does this tell you about Glenda's feelings? How do you interpret Glenda's action? Before you interpret the message, you need to look at the whole situation. What caused the door to slam? Let's look at some possible answers. How does each possibility affect your interpretation of Glenda's action?

For each of the following possibilities, answer these two questions:

- How can you find out if this is the reason for the door slamming?
- How would you react to the door slamming if this is the reason?

Possibility No. 1: Glenda has a habit of slamming doors.

_____

_____

_____

Possibility No. 2: The wind blew the door shut.

_____

_____

_____

Possibility No. 3: Glenda is angry about something or with someone.

_____

_____

_____

Interpreting Body Action

Your point of view affects how you interpret others' body action. The feelings you have for the person committing the actions will influence your interpretation. Perhaps you have heard someone excuse another person's rudeness by saying, "Oh, that's just part of Leonard's personality." But, if someone other than Leonard had done the same thing, that person might have been criticized.

Your point of view is affected by what you have been taught about proper and improper responses. If you have been taught that a particular body action is crude, you will consider the person doing it as crude. However, that person may not have been taught that the action is unacceptable.

Your peers or friends influence your point of view. A social group has acceptable and unacceptable body actions. For example, the reaction of a football team winning a championship isn't the same as a chess team winning a championship. The two groups have different ways of expressing the joy of victory.

Your past life experiences affect your interpretation. If you have seen a certain body action causing a particular reaction, you will expect the same reaction in the future. For example, if a young boy's favorite uncle pats him on the head whenever he comes to visit and then gives him a piece of gum, a pat on the head could suggest a piece of gum to that child.

Check It Out 5-3

Read each of the body actions listed below. Imagine that you are observing these actions. Based on your point of view, interpret each person's action. What message is the person communicating? What emotion is the person expressing? Why is the person using this body action? Write your thoughts for each case.

Body Action | **Your Interpretation**

1. A football player spikes the ball in the end zone.

2. A driver shakes his fist at the driver of a car he is passing.

3. A tennis player throws his racquet on the ground.

4. The club president pounds the desk before the meeting begins.

5. The secretary slams the receiver of the telephone down.

6. The father hugs his son.

7. The auto mechanic kicks the tire of the car.

8. The student breaks his pencil into pieces while taking a test.

9. The police officer holds up his hand in front of a line of cars.

10. The man places his arm on the shoulder of a friend and gives a short squeeze.

Body Language

Another form of nonverbal communication—body language—is more complicated than body actions because it involves more forms of expression. Body language includes

- Hand movements or gestures
- body posture
- Positioning in another person's private space
- Eye contact
- Facial expressions

Knowing how to both use and interpret body language enhances clear communication. Since body language often occurs in connection with spoken language, accurately interpreting body language may tell if a speaker really means what he is saying.

Hand Gestures

Speaking without the use of your hands can be difficult. Some people have been accused of being unable to talk if their hands were tied. Certainly, giving instructions often involves the use of our hands. People tend to point as they indicate a direction such as left or right, up or down.

Hand gestures express a variety of emotions. Anger may be shown when a speaker pounds the table. Being bored may be expressed as a listener unconsciously drums his fingers. At times, a speaker may gain attention by pointing to or touching the listener. A speaker may draw attention to a chart or picture by pointing to it. Gestures such as pulling your hair or biting your fingernails may indicate nervousness.

When interpreting hand gestures, the listener must both observe the gestures and hear the words spoken. The combination of the two is significant because a hand gesture could indicate how strongly the speaker feels about a subject.

A speaker needs to remember that some hand gestures aren't acceptable in a social or business situation. Gestures that indicate vulgar or threatening messages should be avoided. Gesturing this way makes the speaker appear uneducated.

A speaker needs to avoid overusing hand gestures. When a listener becomes too busy looking at a speaker's hands to hear his words, the hands are being overused. Some people have the unconscious habit of pulling on their ear lobe or swinging their arms as they speak. Such gestures distract the listener's attention.

Check It Out 5-4

Study the hand gesture illustrations. What does each gesture tell you that the person is saying? Match each gesture with one of the statements below. Write the correct letter on the line next to the illustration.

A Glad to meet you.
B Who would have thought??
C Point No. 1 is....
D Peace, man.
E I didn't DO it.

F I won!
G Oops! You caught me.
H Hold that pose.
I Reporting for duty, Sir.

Body Posture

Body posture refers to the position of a speaker's body. Is the speaker standing or sitting? Is the speaker standing erect or leaning? Is the speaker sitting behind a desk or in a chair beside the listener?

Each of these body postures sends a message to the listener. The posture may express the speaker's attitude. It might answer such questions as, Who is controlling this meeting? Are the speaker and the listener on an equal basis? Is this a formal or an informal meeting?

The nearness of the speaker to the listener sends a message. As two individuals sit and talk, the speaker leans forward as he discusses an idea. Unconsciously, the speaker is saying, "I really want you to hear this." The listener may cross her arms and lean back indicating, "Convince me! I need more proof before I agree."

Invasion of Personal Space

As the speaker leans forward, the listener may move away from the speaker. All people have an imaginary circle around their bodies that is called their "personal space." When another person enters this space, the first person feels uncomfortable. He usually tries to protect his privacy by moving away from the invader. Unconsciously, the listener is saying, "This is my personal space. Please move out of my personal space."

In the United States, personal space is generally considered to be 36 inches around the body. Personal space means different things to different people in different situations. If you stand in an elevator with one other person, you expect more personal space than you would in an elevator full of people. More or less personal space might be preferred in other countries and cultures (see the later section, "How Culture Affects Nonverbal Communication").

Naturally, the amount of personal space one allows another person to enter varies. A loved one would be allowed much closer than a stranger would be. A friend would be allowed closer than a business acquaintance. Allowing or not allowing another individual to enter your personal space will have a great influence on your communication.

Eye Contact

Eye contact refers to looking at a speaker or a listener. Good eye contact means that you are relaxed and simply looking at the other person's face as you talk. No eye contact means that you are looking out the window, at the floor, or across the room, but not at the person.

Staring would be eye contact used to the extreme to make someone feel uncomfortable.

When a speaker doesn't look at her listener, she sends a message: "I am not comfortable talking to you." The listener interprets this message to fit his own situation. The interpretation might be

- "I can't trust this person. Perhaps she is lying."
- "I can't depend on this person. She isn't confident."
- "This person isn't interested in our conversation."

When a listener doesn't look at the speaker, he sends a message: "I am not interested in listening to you." The speaker interprets this message to fit her own situation. The interpretation might be

- "This person is bored. He isn't interested in this topic."

- "This person doesn't enjoy listening to me."

- "This person is in a hurry. He doesn't have time for me."

Facial Expressions

Facial expressions might be defined as facial gestures. Emotions shown through the use of the eyes, the mouth, and the head are all facial expressions.

Children are often gifted at understanding facial expressions. Watch a child around his mother or father. He will hit his baby brother. Immediately, he will look at his parent's face and wait for a reaction. He might even ask, "Why do you have a mad face?" From his knowledge of facial expressions, he knows that his parent is upset. He looks at his parent and reads the parent's face. He knows he is in trouble without his parent saying anything.

The mouth and the muscles of the face express certain emotions. When you meet a person coming down the street smiling, scowling, or frowning, that facial expression helps you interpret that person's attitude toward life at that particular moment.

The eyes and the muscles around them also communicate emotions. A raised eyebrow shows disapproval, while a wink says, "I'm in on the joke." Tears, rolling eyes, a wide-eyed look, or narrowing of the eyes expresses other emotions.

Motions of the head send messages. Nodding or shaking the head indicates agreement with the speaker. Lowering the head expresses worry or great sadness. Holding the head erect might show defiance. Placing the head in one's hands shows defeat or despair.

Check It Out 5-5

The people illustrated have gathered for the reading of Great Uncle Orville's last will and testament. Uncle Orville's lawyer has just read the will, and each person has inherited a different portion of Uncle Orville's estate.

Observing the facial expressions, select a word from the list below that describes how each person feels about Uncle Orville's gift. Write that emotion below each illustration.

_____

_____

_____

_____

_____

_____

Anger	Skepticism
Happiness	Disappointment
Calmness	Surprise

Culture Affects Nonverbal Communication

Not all cultures use nonverbal communication in the same way. Touching, while acceptable in our society, might not be viewed in the same way in a different culture. If you don't have a cultural background similar to those with whom you are trying to communicate, misunderstandings may result.

A national news broadcast reported just such a misunderstanding. A Korean family had opened a grocery in an area where African-American business people owned the majority of the stores. African-American citizens living in the neighborhood picketed the grocery. The African-American community believed that the Korean grocers were treating them with disrespect. When African-Americans shopped in the grocery, the Koreans didn't look at them. When the Korean cashier made change for purchases, he would lay the coins on the counter. The Korean refused to hand the change to a customer.

The African-Americans were upset with this group of people, who refused to look at them or touch them. However, in the Korean culture, it would have been rude to look at or touch a customer. The misunderstanding resulted from what is acceptable in the African-American culture and the Korean culture.

Even if your cultural background differs from the world in which you must communicate, you still must be able to function in that world. You may need to learn some different nonverbal communication skills in order to be successful.

Check Your Vocabulary

Read the vocabulary list. These words appear in this chapter. Read the following definitions, and place the letter of the correct word on the line in front of the definition.

A	nonverbal communication	E	body posture
B	body language	F	eye contact
C	hand gestures	G	personal space
D	facial expressions	H	body action

1. _____ Movements of the hands used to express a speaker's feelings.

2. _____ The position of the speaker's body.

3. _____ Looking at a speaker or listener while communicating.

4. _____ An invisible circle surrounding a person's body and considered an area of privacy.

5. _____ Gestures involving the eyes, mouth, and head.

6. _____ Hand gestures, facial expressions, body posture, and eye contact used to express emotions without speaking.

7. _____ The movement of a part of the body that expresses an emotion. For example, tapping one's foot might express impatience with another person.

8. _____ Sending and receiving messages without using spoken words.

Summing It Up

Nonverbal communication takes place without words. Body action is a type of nonverbal communication in which emotions are shown through the use of the body. Some types of body action aren't acceptable. Therefore, the messenger must control his body actions.

Body language is another type of nonverbal communication. Body language includes the use of hand gestures, eye contact, body posture, and facial expressions. Nonverbal communication takes place constantly as people observe each other and interpret the meaning of their actions.

Childhood teaching, social groups, and past experiences affect the way people view the actions of others. A person's cultural background also influences this interpretation. To communicate effectively, one must learn to interpret nonverbal communication using the standards of the culture in which you live.

Remember, you communicate even when no words are spoken. Learn to use nonverbal communication effectively to express your thoughts. Just as importantly, learn to understand the nonverbal communication of those around you. You will become more effective as you practice these skills.

CHAPTER 6

Written Communication

Written communication includes notes, letters, and memos. Remember, only 8.4 percent of communicating is done through writing. However, knowing how to communicate through writing remains an important communication skill.

Writing involves knowing how to use words correctly. The combination of words chosen affects the meaning of the written communication. Punctuation is also essential in writing a message that can be clearly understood. These skills are usually taught in English composition classes.

Why Is Writing Important?

Written communication can make language clearer. Oral communication isn't always clearly understood. Some words have more than one meaning. This can cause confusion.

An old riddle asks the question, "What is black and white and *read* all over?" The answer is a newspaper. The same riddle may be asked, "What is black and white and *red* all over?" The answer is a blushing zebra.

The way one writes the italicized word makes the difference in the answer to this riddle. When a speaker communicates the riddle orally, the listener can't be sure if the speaker means the color word "red" or the action word "read." When the word is communicated through writing, the meaning of the word is clear. When writing, a person must focus on each individual word. With this focus, the meaning of each word becomes more important. The writer concentrates more on clear expression. When speaking, our words often aren't as thoughtfully expressed.

Writing puts communication in a form that can be kept. Sometimes, communication needs to be saved for future reference. Written communication makes this possible. Some written communication, such as old love letters or historic documents, becomes valuable as years pass. Documents such as the Declaration of Independence or the Constitution remind us of our national heritage. Grandma and Grandpa's diaries hidden away in the attic remind us of our family roots.

Written communication acts as a reminder of oral communication or of legal, business, or other person-to-person transactions. The minutes of an organization's meetings remind the members what happened at the previous meeting. "Get it in writing" is good advice in the case of an agreement between two people. What has been agreed upon orally can be written in a contract. This written agreement signed by two parties becomes legally binding.

Telephone, Computer, or Letter?

You may handle your personal business in many different ways. You can write a letter or an e-mail to send a consumer complaint. You can fax a catalog order or call it in. With a computer, you can contact a company Web site to view product lines, check banking and other accounts, and even apply for a job. Shopping using the Internet saves time for many people. But sometimes Web sites aren't accessible, computers shut down, and e-mail isn't read.

Knowing when to telephone, when to use your computer, and when to write a business letter will save you time and frustration as you manage your personal business.

The telephone is a handy way to conduct personal business. You can talk directly to a person and get answers your questions immediately. If something isn't clear, you can ask another question until you fully understand.

However, a telephone is not always the best way to handle personal business. You may not be able to reach an individual. Perhaps a secretary tells you that the person isn't accessible or that the person doesn't answer her telephone. Then, a letter may be the better choice for communicating. A letter will be delivered to the individual when a telephone call won't do the job.

The Advantages of Letter Writing

Some businesses don't want their telephone lines tied up with outside calls. For instance, many job advertisements request "No Phone Calls"; job applications will only be taken by letter. Often businesses need your signature on a letter as proof that you have made a particular request. An example of this might be your wish to cancel an insurance policy.

If you are trying to resolve a very complicated problem, a letter may be the better choice. As you write the letter, you can explain your thoughts in a step-by-step procedure. The problem may be more clearly understood after you have organized it on paper.

Sometimes an e-mail or a telephone call, plus a letter would be a good idea. A letter may be used to confirm information discussed in a telephone conversation or to expand a short e-mail message. A telephone call or an e-mail may notify someone that a letter is being sent to confirm the receipt.

Written Communication in Your Personal Life

A personal letter is a friendly communication written to someone you know. Simply written, it contains personal news and shares mutual interests between friends. A letter may be the only way you have of keeping in touch with a friend. Friends in the armed services or away at college, or those who have moved away from your area, welcome a personal letter. A letter says, "I thought about you today. You are important to me. See, I took time to write you this letter."

A personal letter consists of five parts. Each part has a special purpose. Look at the following sample copy of a personal letter.

A Sample Personal Letter

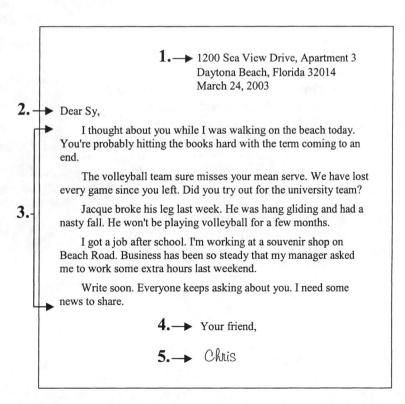

1. → 1200 Sea View Drive, Apartment 3
Daytona Beach, Florida 32014
March 24, 2003

2. → Dear Sy,

I thought about you while I was walking on the beach today. You're probably hitting the books hard with the term coming to an end.

The volleyball team sure misses your mean serve. We have lost every game since you left. Did you try out for the university team?

3. Jacque broke his leg last week. He was hang gliding and had a nasty fall. He won't be playing volleyball for a few months.

I got a job after school. I'm working at a souvenir shop on Beach Road. Business has been so steady that my manager asked me to work some extra hours last weekend.

Write soon. Everyone keeps asking about you. I need some news to share.

4. → Your friend,

5. → Chris

Heading

Look at the part of the personal letter labeled number 1. Called the heading, it contains the address of the writer and the current date. The address includes the street address and a box number or apartment number; depending on your situation, all or only some of these may be a part of your address. This part of the address is written on the first line of the heading. Each word of the address begins with a capital letter.

The second line of the heading contains the city, state, and ZIP code. The first letter of each word in the city and state names are capitalized. A comma is placed after the city.

The current date (month, day, and year) is written on the last line of the heading. The month must begin with a capital letter. A comma is placed after the day.

Salutation or Greeting

Part 2 of the personal letter—the salutation, or greeting—is simply a way of saying "hello" to the person that you're writing. Usually, the greeting is written as "Dear Susan." Each word of the greeting begins with a capital letter. A comma follows the last word.

Body

Part 3 of a personal letter, the body, is the main part of the letter. It covers the news and information being written to your friend. The body of the letter may be a few paragraphs or several pages long.

Closing

Part 4 of a personal letter, the closing, ends the letter. Closing phrases might include "With love" or "As ever" or "Sincerely." The choice depends on what is appropriate to the relationship of the writer and recipient and to the mood of the letter. The first word of the closing begins with a capital letter. A comma follows the last word.

Signature

Part 5 of a personal letter is the writer's handwritten signature. If the letter is to a close friend, only the first name is written. At times, the writer's full name may be written.

Check It Out	**6-1**

Your best friend has moved to a city 500 miles away from your home. On a separate sheet of paper, write a letter telling your friend about some of the things that have been happening in your community and with your friends. Use the correct form for a personal letter.

When you have finished the letter, be sure to proofread it. Check to make sure you have used the correct spelling, grammar, and punctuation. Label the five parts of your personal letter.

Thank-You Notes

Another type of personal communication is a thank-you note. It isn't as long as a letter. It is just a short paragraph or two written to thank someone for a gift, sent as a courteous response to someone else's thoughtfulness. If a gift has been sent to you, a thank-you note lets the sender know that you have received the gift.

A bread-and-butter note is much like a thank-you note. It is written to thank someone for something done for you. This might include a lunch invitation, taking you to the theater, or having you spend the weekend. Such short notes are written soon after the event. The term "bread-and-butter" probably came from the fact that such a note is often written to thank someone for a dinner invitation.

The note should say something about the gift or the thoughtful act. If the gift was money, the amount of money doesn't need to be written. However, telling what you plan to do with the money would be proper.

A Sample Thank-You Note

> 223 Charles Street
> Spring Valley, Ohio 45370
> August 17, 2003
>
> Dear Maria,
>
> I was so surprised to get the painting you sent. Since we moved, I have been looking for something to hang in the living room. The colors in the painting match the living room perfectly.
>
> I'm so proud to tell all my visitors that my talented friend, Maria, painted it just for me. Thank you so much. I can't wait till you can see where I placed it.
>
> Sincerely,
>
> *Brittany*

Effective Communication Skills

Your grandparents are moving from their large home to a small apartment. They have given you an antique chest that you have always admired. Write a thank-you note to them. Use the correct form for a thank-you note.

After writing the note, proofread it. Check the spelling, punctuation, and grammar. Label the five parts of the thank-you note.

Invitations

Another type of personal written communication, an invitation is a short note asking another person to do something with you. It might be an invitation to a party or a wedding, or to go snowboarding.

To avoid confusion, an invitation must answer certain questions about the event. The questions that need answers will depend on the event. Look at the following questions that invitations often address:

- **Who?** Who is in charge of this event and extending the invitation?

- **What?** Is this a formal or casual party, a dinner, an open house, a carry-in, a picnic? Is it for adults only or a family event?

- **When?** When will this event take place? What day of the week? What date? At what time of day will it start? When will it end? (The hours need to be listed.)

- **Where?** Where will this event take place? What is the name of the location? What is the address? Do directions need to be included?

- **Why?** What is the reason for this event? Is the event to honor someone? Are gifts appropriate or inappropriate? Is it a celebration just for fun?

Often at the end of an invitation, the term "R.S.V.P." is written. These letters indicate that a reply to the invitation is expected. The writer is asking that you simply tell him "Yes, I'm coming" or "No, I won't be able to come." If a host needs to know how much food to prepare or how many cars are needed to get everyone to the ski lodge, this is a way of finding out. The "R.S.V.P." may include a telephone number for people to call when they reply. Here is a sample invitation.

Sample Invitation 1

904 Tweedle Lane
Garden City, ID 83704
May 7, 2003

Dear Carlos,

I am writing to invite you to the next meeting of the Computer User's Group. A guest speaker will be talking about using printers with your computer. The meeting will be held in the basement of the Community Hall from 7:30-9:00 p.m. on Thursday, May 23. I hope to see you there.

Sincerely,

Don Freeman

Don Freeman

✓ Check It Out 6-3

Using Sample Invitation 1, answer the following questions about the meeting that Carlos is being invited to.

Who is in charge of the event? _____

What? _____

When? _____

Where? _____

Why? _____

An invitation may also be written as a form. Look at the following sample invitation.

Sample Invitation 2

Come to a Retirement Party
Honoring Our Friend and Co-worker
🔖 **Pauline** 🔖

Name: Pauline Woods
Place: Old Stone House Restaurant
1455 Stony Road
Date: January 28
Time: Noon
R.S.V.P.: Jenny Miller, 594-7602

Check It Out 6-4

Using Sample Invitation 2, answer the following questions about the party.

Who is extending the invitation? _____

What? _____

When? _____

Where? _____

Why? _____

| **Check It Out** | **6-5** |

You are planning a surprise birthday party for your best friend. Write an invitation to the party. Use the letter format shown in Sample Invitation 1.

After you have written the invitation, proofread it. Check the spelling, grammar, and punctuation. Using your invitation, answer the following questions.

Who is extending the invitation? _____

What? _____

When? _____

Where? _____

Why? _____

Using the same information, write the invitation in the form used in Sample Invitation 2.

When you have completed the invitation, proofread it. Using the invitation, answer the following questions.

Who is extending the invitation? _____

What? _____

When? _____

Where? _____

Why? _____

Written Communication in Your Business Life

Each person needs to know the skill of writing a business letter. A business letter can be written requesting a new appliance part. Perhaps you buy a product that doesn't work properly. You need to write a letter requesting a refund or a replacement for it. You want to know how to apply to a technical school program in another state. A letter needs to be written asking for this material. You include a business cover letter when sending a resume to a prospective employer.

The Parts of a Business Letter

A business letter consists of six parts. Look at the following sample.

Sample Business Letter 1

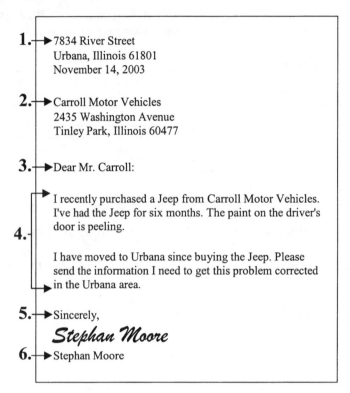

1. → 7834 River Street
Urbana, Illinois 61801
November 14, 2003

2. → Carroll Motor Vehicles
2435 Washington Avenue
Tinley Park, Illinois 60477

3. → Dear Mr. Carroll:

4. I recently purchased a Jeep from Carroll Motor Vehicles. I've had the Jeep for six months. The paint on the driver's door is peeling.

I have moved to Urbana since buying the Jeep. Please send the information I need to get this problem corrected in the Urbana area.

5. → Sincerely,

Stephan Moore

6. → Stephan Moore

Heading

Look at the part of the business letter labeled 1. This heading consists of the writer's address and the current date. A comma is placed after the name of the city. Also, a comma is placed after the day in the date. Each word in the heading is capitalized.

Inside Address

Part 2 of a business letter is the inside address. This is the address of the person or business being contacted. The first line of the inside address is the name of the person or organization. This is followed by the business address. The punctuation should follow the same style used in the heading. Each word in the inside address is capitalized.

Salutation

The salutation is part 3 of a business letter. This is the greeting to the person receiving the letter. If a person's name is not available to use in the salutation, the company's name may be used; for example, "Dear Dearskin Company:". Notice that the salutation is followed by a colon (:). The salutation in a personal letter is followed by comma.

Body

Part 4, the body, is the message of the business letter. It should express the writer's request or opinion in a few short paragraphs.

Closing

The closing, part 5 of a business letter, ends the letter. Closings that may be used in a business letter include "Sincerely yours," or "Cordially," or "Yours truly,". Notice that the first word of the closing is capitalized. A comma follows the last word.

Signature

Part 6 of a business letter is the signature. The writer's full name is both typed and signed.

Sample Business Letter 2

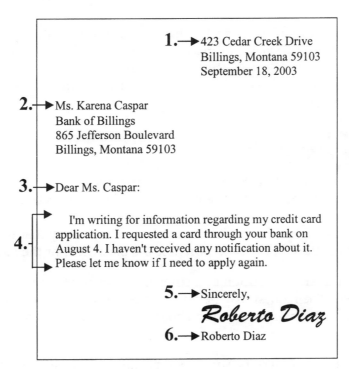

The Look of a Business Letter

A business letter is more formal than a personal letter. Because a business receives many letters each day, a short letter will receive attention more quickly. This means that the writer needs to express his message using as few sentences as possible. A business letter is often only a page in length.

If typed, a business letter may be written in block form or modified block form. If hand-writing a business letter, use the modified block form.

Sample Business Letter 1 is typed using block form. This means that all parts of the letter start on the left side of the page. The paragraphs are not indented, and double spacing separates the paragraphs.

The modified block form, shown in Sample Business Letter 2, uses indented paragraphs. The closing and the signature line up with the heading.

When typing a business letter, leave four spaces between the closing and the typed signature. This allows space for the written signature. If the letter is handwritten, just sign the letter.

It is wise to keep a copy of a business letter for your own information. Referring to the copy, you will know exactly what information you wrote to the company if some question arises about your letter. Because the date is a part of the heading, you will know how long it has been since you contacted the company. The inside address will help you if you need to write the company again.

A Letter of Request

A letter of request is written to a company for information about their product. Sometimes, a customer buys a product that requires assembly. If instructions or parts are missing, the customer should write a letter of request. Or perhaps a customer has purchased a product in the past; the product has been so satisfactory that the customer wants current information on where to purchase a replacement or the latest model.

A letter of request can also be written to a company or organization asking about the services it offers. The request may be for advanced tickets to a play or sports event. A letter of request might seek information about the prices charged for camping in a state park.

When writing a letter of request, be sure to supply all the information such as code numbers for parts needed, the number of tickets you are ordering, or a description of the item you are wanting to replace.

Be sure to send your request to the correct address. If you don't have a department or a person to address, send the letter to Customer Service. If you don't know the address, the telephone directory's yellow pages would be a place to look. If the business is outside your local calling area, advertisements might be helpful. Instruction manuals that come with appliances and tools often contain addresses. The local library or the Internet would be other sources for obtaining a business address.

Choose a city that you would like to visit on vacation. Write to the Chamber of Commerce in that city. Ask for vacation information including local sights, entertainment, and motel accommodations. Use the proper business form.

When you have finished the letter, proofread it. Check the spelling, punctuation, and grammar. Label the six parts of a business letter.

A Job Application Letter

A job seeker may write a letter to a business or company requesting information about a job opening. This letter may simply ask for a job application. Many companies place advertisements in the help wanted section of the newspaper or a magazine regarding a job opening.

At other times, a letter is written as an inquiry to a company. In this letter, the writer would give information about himself to inquire if the company is interested in someone with his qualifications. This letter would be written in business letter form. A resume listing the writer's past work experience would be included with the letter. This type of business letter is called a cover letter.

Read the following advertisement.

> ## TRAVEL AGENTS WANTED
> ### Opening New Downtown Office
> #### Now hiring 3 new travel agents
> Send letter to:
> ## KNAPSACK TRAVEL, INC.
> ## PO BOX 364
> ## SACRAMENTO, CA 95814

You have just completed a travel course. Write a business letter to Knapsack Travel asking for an application.

When you have finished the letter, proofread it. Check the spelling, punctuation, and grammar. Label the six parts of a business letter.

A Consumer Complaint Letter

A product doesn't work the way the manufacturer claims it will. An appliance breaks while it is still under the guarantee. The credit card company sends a bill for an item that was returned to the store. In these cases, the customer may write a letter of consumer complaint. The writer may request that the company replace the product or that the purchase price of the product be refunded.

A letter of consumer complaint should clearly state the problem. The letter should be written firmly but without angry words.

The letter should be addressed to the Customer Service Department of the company. If you are dealing with a billing problem, you can usually find a Customer Service address somewhere on the bill. If you have a complaint with a product, check the box that the product came in or the information booklet that came with the product for the address of the company. An information booklet may also provide instructions on how to return the product. Another source would be the company's Web site.

Check It Out 6-8

You belong to the Video-of-the-Month Club; 223 King Avenue; Waterloo, Iowa 50701. Each month you order a video, which arrives at your home. This month your selection was "Bigfoot Goes to Hawaii." Someone made a mistake. You got "Big Wig Goes to Harvard" instead.

Write a letter of consumer complaint to the video club. When you finish the letter, proofread it. Check the spelling, punctuation, and grammar. Label the six parts of a business letter.

Check Your Vocabulary

Read the vocabulary list. These words appear in this chapter. Read the following definitions, and place the number of the correct word on the line in front of the definition.

A personal letter
B heading
C business letter
D inside address
E salutation
F body
G closing
H signature
I thank-you note

J bread-and-butter note
K invitation
L R.S.V.P.
M block form
N modified block form
O letter of request
P letter of consumer complaint
Q letter of job application

1. _____ An abbreviation used on an invitation asking the receiver to reply whether he will or won't attend a special event.

2. _____ A friendly letter written to someone telling personal news.

3. _____ The main part of a letter; the message.

4. _____ A short letter written as a courtesy thanking someone for a gift.

5. _____ Part of a letter; the writer's name.

6. _____ A short letter written to ask someone to a special event.

7. _____ The first part of a letter consisting of the writer's address and the current date.

8. _____ A letter written to a company or organization.

9. _____ A short thank-you letter written to someone for a special kindness.

10. _____ The part of a letter indicating the end of the letter.

11. _____ A business letter written in a form with all parts of the letter starting on the left side of the page.

12. _____ The greeting at the beginning of a letter.

13. _____ A business letter asking for information about a company's product or services.

14. _____ A business letter written to inquire about a job or possible job.

15. _____ A business letter written with indented paragraphs and the closing and signature lined up with the heading.

16. _____ The part of a business letter containing the name and address of the company or organization being written.

17. _____ A business letter written to a company or organization stating a request or complaint by a customer of the company.

Summing It Up

Learning to write well will help you communicate with friends and acquaintances. Through personal letters, you can share news with friends, express your gratitude in a thank-you note, and offer hospitality with an invitation to a special occasion. As you learn to write clearly, you will feel more confidence in social situations.

You will need to write business letters many times in your life. Reasons for writing a business letter include applying for a job, requesting information, getting an item repaired, or correcting a billing error.

A business letter should contain all six parts: the heading, the inside address, the salutation, the body, the closing, and the signature. A business letter should be written clearly with only a few paragraphs explaining the reason for the letter.

It is a good idea to keep a copy of a business letter. This allows you to see what you have written if the company has questions or needs more information. It also tells you when you sent the letter to the company.

CHAPTER 7

Getting a Letter to Its Destination

Much thought and effort goes into writing a letter. Whether you write a letter to a friend telling about your latest wacky adventures or to a company asking for better service, you want that letter to reach its destination. Part of written communication involves knowing how to properly prepare a letter to be mailed.

The United States Postal Service delivers 200 billion pieces of mail each year. If you prepare your letter properly for mailing, it should arrive at its destination safely and quickly. If the letter isn't properly prepared, the Postal Service may be slower in delivery or may not be able to deliver it at all.

The Parts of the Envelope

Look at the sample envelope below.

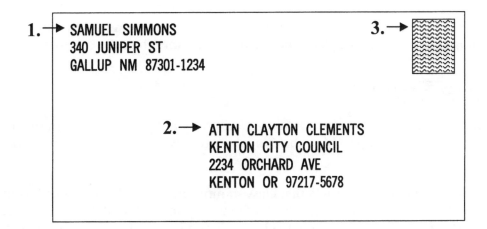

Return Address

Part 1 of the envelope is called the return address. This is the address of the letter writer. If for some reason the Postal Service is unable to deliver a letter, it will send the letter back to its return address. Without a return address, the letter would simply be a lost piece of mail. Always use a return address.

Place the return address in the upper-left corner of the envelope. The return address is written in block form, that is, the left side of each line lines up with the left side of the line above it.

The top line of the return address is the sender's name. The next line is the street address, the rural route, or post office box; this is followed by any apartment or office number. The last line of the return address holds the city, state, and ZIP+4 code.

Destination Address

Part 2 of the envelope, the destination address, shows where the letter is being mailed.

The destination address is written in block form. Each line is placed directly below the previous line, aligning on the left side. The top line of the destination address should be the receiver's name. This could be a person, an organization, or a business.

Sometimes, the envelope is addressed to a company or organization. An "Attention" line can be added if a particular person in the company is being addressed. Place an "Attention" line above the name of the organization or business name.

The next line is the street address, the rural route, or post office box. This is followed by an apartment, unit, office, or other number, if needed.

The last line is the city, state, and ZIP+4 code. If the letter is going to another country, only the country's name should be written in full as the last item in the address. The foreign postal code should be placed beside the city, rather than the country.

Postage Stamp

Part 3 of the envelope is the postage stamp. Don't forget to put the stamp in the upper-right corner of the envelope. Using the correct postage will ensure that your letter gets delivered.

Most letters may be mailed using a first class stamp, sold by the United States Postal Service. If a letter has several pages, it may weigh more than the Postal Service will deliver using a first class stamp. In this case, the letter should be taken to the post office, where a postal clerk will weigh the letter. The postal clerk will tell you the cost of any additional postage needed. If a letter is being sent to someone outside of the United States, the post office will tell you what postage is needed. A postage stamp will be put in the top-right corner of the envelope. This indicates that you paid the postage cost. A letter mailed without the correct amount of postage will be returned to you.

Computerized Mail Processing

The Postal Service increasingly uses automation in processing the mail. Automation is the use of machines to do the work of people. As machines are used, fewer people are sorting the mail. Machines such as optical character readers (OCRs) and barcode sorters (BCSs) increase the speed, efficiency, and accuracy of mail delivery. These machines can sort up to 36,000 pieces of mail each hour. Every second, these computerized processes can sort 10 pieces of mail. Postal centers throughout the United States use this equipment. Chances are that your mail is processed this way.

In the process the destination address will be "read," and the OCR printer will spray a bar code representing the delivery address on the lower-right corner of the envelope. Then the OCR sorts barcoded letters according to their delivery areas. This mail is fed into a barcode sorter, which separates it further by mail carrier routes for delivery.

Since machines don't think, the way that you prepare your mail is very important. Your mail needs to be both machineable and readable. Machineable means that the size and the shape of the mail allows it to pass through the processing equipment without problems. Readable mail can be quickly and accurately read, coded, and sorted by the machines.

Envelopes: Size Makes a Difference

Rectangular envelopes should be used for mailing letters. An envelope should be no smaller than 3 1/2 inches by 5 inches; otherwise, it is not mailable. It should be no larger than 6 1/8 inches by 11 1/2 inches. Envelopes that are larger than this can be mailed, but can't be sorted by the automated equipment, delaying delivery.

Business-size envelopes measure 4 1/4 inches by 9 1/2 inches, which fits the mailable range. Commonly called Size 10 or Number 10 envelopes, they can be purchased in the office supply department of many stores.

Color and Print Make a Difference

The color of the envelope and the color of the ink used to write the address should contrast strongly. The OCR works best when reading black type or ink on a white envelope. Other color combinations will work; however, for best results, the ink should be as dark as possible and the background as light as possible. Avoid addressing envelopes in unusual colors or pencil.

Sloppy handwriting can confuse an OCR. Misreadings can also be caused by unusual printing styles, or if extra words or business logos show within the address block on the envelope.

Address Location Makes a Difference

To be read by the OCR, all lines of the destination address should be placed within what is called the OCR read area. This rectangular space on each envelope starts 2 3/4 inches from the top of the envelope. It ends 5/8 inches from the bottom. This allows room for the Postal Service to place the barcode below the destination address. No part of the return address should be placed in the OCR read area. Any logo or extra design on the envelope should be above this rectangle.

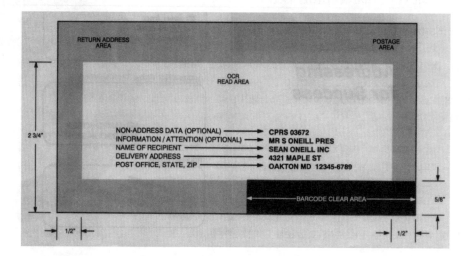

Addressing an Envelope

Addressing an envelope correctly helps ensure delivery. Make the address as complete as you possibly can. This means including apartment and suite numbers.

Use the correct delivery designations such as ST (street), RD (road), or BLVD (boulevard). (See the discussion of common abbreviations in next section.) Is the address Cherry Street, Cherry Lane, or Cherry Drive? Some cities may have all three places in their postal area.

Directions are sometimes a part of the delivery designation, such as NW (northwest) or S (south). In a large city, North Park Avenue may be many miles from South Park Avenue. The two areas may not even be served by the same postal station.

Use the following basic form in setting up the address. You may need to change this if the address contains additional information.

- Line 1: Attention line (if needed)
- Line 2: Name of organization or person (title of individual, if needed)

- Line 3: Street address, rural route or post office box number, apartment, office, unit or suite number (if needed)
- Line 4: City, state, ZIP+4 code

Make It Machine-Readable

Be sure to write the address clearly. If you are handwriting the address, printing may be best. Write the address in block form. Remember that elaborate letters can confuse an OCR. Plain block letters or a simple type is the best choice.

Use capital letters throughout the address. The only punctuation is a hyphen in the ZIP+4 code. Whenever possible, use the common address and state abbreviations listed later in this section, before "Check It Out 7-2."

Note: What? No comma between the city and state? Yes! According to the United States Postal Service, a comma or period can confuse the OCR. The only punctuation you should use is the hyphen between the ZIP code and the ZIP+4 numbers.

If an OCR doesn't see a space between characters and words, it assumes that they are all connected. So you must be put spaces between words. This space must be at least the width of a printed letter "M". In addition, each line of the address needs its own specific horizontal space to indicate a different line in the address.

Have the Right "Delivery Line"

The automated equipment "reads" the line immediately above the city, state, and ZIP+4 code line, which is called the delivery line. The mail will be delivered to that address.

If the delivery line is too long to be written on only one line, place the information such as the apartment number or box number on the line above the street address. This will enable a quicker delivery.

Some companies have both a street address and a post office box at another street location. The Postal Service will deliver to either the street address or the box number, depending on which appears above the city, state, and ZIP+4 code line.

Use ZIP+4 for Accuracy

The ZIP code is a five-digit number given to a postal delivery area. Be sure to use the correct ZIP code. A letter with an incorrect ZIP code will be sent to a different area, slowing delivery. If you don't know the ZIP code, check with the post office. Booklets listing ZIP codes are available, or you can check the list at the Postal Service Web site (www.usps.com).

In 1983, the Postal Service added four additional numbers to the original ZIP codes. This is called ZIP+4. The four-digit add-on number code represents a geographical part of the delivery area. This could be a city block, an office building, or an individual who receives a great deal of mail.

Using ZIP+4 is not required for mail delivery. Its use is voluntary. However, the Postal Service says that mail will be delivered more accurately if ZIP+4 is used. So if you know the ZIP+4 code, you may want to use it.

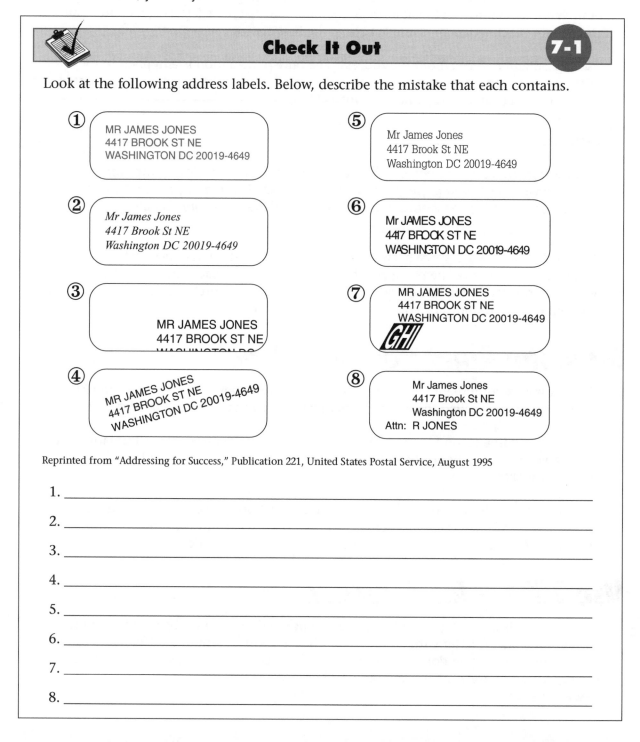

Check It Out 7-1

Look at the following address labels. Below, describe the mistake that each contains.

① MR JAMES JONES
4417 BROOK ST NE
WASHINGTON DC 20019-4649

② *Mr James Jones*
4417 Brook St NE
Washington DC 20019-4649

③ MR JAMES JONES
4417 BROOK ST NE
WASHINGTON DC

④ MR JAMES JONES
4417 BROOK ST NE
WASHINGTON DC 20019-4649

⑤ Mr James Jones
4417 Brook St NE
Washington DC 20019-4649

⑥ Mr JAMES JONES
4417 BROOK ST NE
WASHINGTON DC 20019-4649

⑦ MR JAMES JONES
4417 BROOK ST NE
WASHINGTON DC 20019-4649
GHI

⑧ Mr James Jones
4417 Brook St NE
Washington DC 20019-4649
Attn: R JONES

Reprinted from "Addressing for Success," Publication 221, United States Postal Service, August 1995

1. _____
2. _____
3. _____
4. _____
5. _____
6. _____
7. _____
8. _____

Address Abbreviations

The following abbreviations are commonly accepted by the United States Postal Service.

State Abbreviations

Alabama	AL	Kentucky	KY	North Dakota	ND
Alaska	AK	Louisiana	LA	Ohio	OH
Arizona	AZ	Maine	ME	Oklahoma	OK
Arkansas	AR	Maryland	MD	Oregon	OR
California	CA	Massachusetts	MA	Pennsylvania	PA
Colorado	CO	Michigan	MI	Rhode Island	RI
Connecticut	CT	Minnesota	MN	South Carolina	SC
Delaware	DE	Mississippi	MS	South Dakota	SD
District of Columbia	DC	Missouri	MO	Tennessee	TN
Florida	FL	Montana	MT	Texas	TX
Georgia	GA	Nebraska	NE	Utah	UT
Hawaii	HI	Nevada	NV	Vermont	VT
Idaho	ID	New Hampshire	NH	Virginia	VA
Illinois	IL	New Jersey	NJ	Washington	WA
Indiana	IN	New Mexico	NM	West Virginia	WV
Iowa	IA	New York	NY	Wisconsin	WI
Kansas	KS	North Carolina	NC	Wyoming	WY

United States	US

Common Address Abbreviations

Apartment	APT	Hospital	HOSP	Road	RD
Attention	ATTN	Island	IS	Room	RM
Avenue	AVE	Junction	JCT	Rural Route	RR
Beach	BCH	Lane	LN	South	S
Boulevard	BLVD	Mount	MT	Southeast	SE
Building	BLDG	Mountain	MTN	Southwest	SW
Center	CTR	North	N	Station	STA
Court	CT	Northeast	NE	Street	ST
Department	DEPT	Northwest	NW	Suite	STE
Drive	DR	Parkway	PKY	Terrace	TER
East	E	Place	PL	Turnpike	TPKE
Expressway	EXPY	Plaza	PLZ	Unit	UNIT
Floor	FL	President	PRES	Valley	VLY
Heights	HTS	Post Office Box	PO BOX	West	W
Highway	HWY				

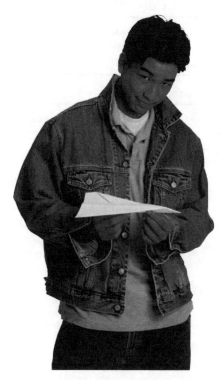

| **Check It Out** | **7-2** |

You will need six business-size envelopes. Using the following information, practice addressing envelopes. Use the address and state abbreviations listed previously. Use the proper form.

Sender	Receiver
1. You	Mrs. Char Hawthorne representing Wall Realty in Topeka, Kansas 66603-1234 at 869 East Silver Street
2. Joan Smythe of Walden, Vermont 05869-5678 who lives at 22 Evergreen Valley, Apartment 7B	Cecil Turnover at 789 Sprint Road in Sunset, Texas 76270-8901
3. You	George Washington lives at Mount Vernon, Virginia. The ZIP code is 22121-3456. He resides at 1776 Cherry Lane. He is President of the United States.
4. Betsy Frazier, Rural Route 4, in Snowball, Arkansas 72676-5432	Neal Madison in Highland, Minnesota 55411-2332 at 3400 South Merrill Drive
5. You	Yellowtail State Park in Yellowtail, Montana 59035-5678 at Post Office Box 451. You want the attention of the head ranger.
6. James Roberts of Parker, Georgia 30316-4321 at 5400 Normal Boulevard	Cedarville Hospital, Dr. Kelly Fuller, Suite 327, 7812 North Medical Plaza, Cedarville, Ohio 45314-3456

Preparing a Letter for Mailing

Fold a letter neatly before placing it in the envelope. A letter is usually folded into thirds.

Place the letter in the envelope. Be sure to seal the envelope. The envelope will be traveling through many postal bags, bins, and machines before it arrives at its destination. If it isn't sealed properly, the envelope may come open. The letter may fall out of the envelope and be lost before it reaches its destination.

 Check It Out 7-3

Using a piece of notebook paper, follow the directions to properly fold a letter.

1. Start with the bottom of the letter. Fold it toward the top of the letter. Place the bottom of the page on the paper so that you can see one-third of the letter at the top. (See the dotted line on the illustration.)

2. Fold the top of the letter over the part of the letter you have already folded. (This fold would be the dotted line on the illustration.) Crease the folds before placing the letter in the envelope.

Top

- - - - - - - - - - - - - - - - - - -

Bottom

> Some companies use self-addressed envelopes for their customers' use in paying bills or making other business replies. Sometimes these business envelopes have a window in the OCR read area. When placing a billing receipt or any other form in a window envelope, you need to make sure that the complete address can be seen through the window. If you can't see the address, the OCR can't "read" the information, and the mail will be returned to the sender.

Check Your Vocabulary

Read the vocabulary list. These words appear in this chapter. Read the following definitions, and place the letter of the correct word on the line in front of the definition.

A	United States Postal Service	I	postage stamp
B	address abbreviations	J	delivery line
C	return address	K	postal clerk
D	attention line	L	OCR
E	destination address	M	readable mail
F	ZIP code	N	BCS
G	automation	O	machineable mail
H	ZIP+4		

1. _____ The person working behind the desk at the local post office.

2. _____ Optical character reader, a machine that is used to spray a barcode on mail to speed up mail delivery.

3. _____ A line in the address stating that a particular person in the organization needs to see this piece of mail.

4. _____ A five-digit number used to sort mail to a particular postal delivery area.

5. _____ The use of machines to do the work of people.

6. _____ The agency responsible for delivering mail throughout the United States.

7. _____ Envelopes that are the right size and shape to pass through automated postal equipment used to process mail.

8. _____ The line in the address above the city, state, and ZIP code.

9. _____ The 5-digit ZIP code with a 4-digit add-on number used to identify a particular office building, city block, or individual receiving a large amount of mail within a postal delivery area.

10. _____ The sender's address on the envelope; written in the top-left corner of the envelope.

11. _____ A stamp sold by the Postal Service and placed in the top-right corner of the envelope.

12. _____ Barcode sorter; an automated machine that sorts mail that has been barcoded and then delivers it to letter carriers for delivery.

13. _____ The address to which a letter is being mailed.

14. _____ Shortened forms of words used in an address.

15. _____ Mail that has been addressed so that it is easily read, coded, and sorted by computerized postal machines.

Summing It Up

Getting a letter to its destination is easy if you follow some simple rules. Remember these basic rules to get your letter there.

Addressing Rules

- Use the proper size envelope.

- Fold the letter neatly before placing it in the envelope.

- Seal the envelope.

- Write the address neatly. Use the proper form and correct abbreviations. Be sure to include the ZIP code or ZIP+4, if possible.

- Always put the return address in the top-left corner of the envelope.

- Don't forget the stamp. Place it in the top-right corner of the envelope.

- If you have a question about addressing or postage, ask the postal clerk at the local post office.

CHAPTER 8

Communicating Using Technology

Technology has greatly affected the way people communicate. In today's world, both businesses and individuals receive and send memos, personal messages, and even documents via fax machines and electronic mail.

Communicating with someone on the other side of the world within minutes rather than days isn't considered unusual any more. With the right equipment, you can easily "chat" with someone in Australia as if you were talking to your next door neighbor. Legal documents can be faxed from one part of the country to another. Knowing how to use technology in communicating is an important skill.

Just Fax It to Me

What does it mean to fax information? A fax machine uses a telephone line to send a document to another fax machine. Depending on the telephone lines, this could be across town or from the East Coast to the West Coast.

As with using a telephone, both the sender and the receiver must have a fax machine. Each fax machine has its own fax number. It consists of an area code, a three-digit prefix, plus a four-number sequence.

Imagine that you needed to fax your signed movie contract to a theatrical agent in Hollywood. First, you would place the signed contract in your fax machine. Next, you would pick up the fax phone receiver and dial your agent's fax number. You would hear a high-pitched sound. This tells you to start "faxing."

When you push the start button on your fax machine, the fax translates the image of the contract's written words into electrical signals. These are transmitted through the telephone system to the fax machine in Hollywood. The fax machine in Hollywood translates this electrical code back into a visual image and prints the document. As your contract passes through your fax machine, an exact duplicate is coming out of the fax machine in Hollywood. Business technology makes you a Hollywood star.

The Advantages of Faxing

Like a telephone, a fax machine offers the convenience of speed. Contact is immediate. It gives a person a paper copy without any delay. When someone needs signed documents, a fax offers a fast way to send the documents and retrieve a signed copy. Documents that once needed to be packaged and sent in overnight mail may now be faxed and arrive within a few minutes. A customer's order can be delivered quicker when it is placed using a fax machine.

A fax machine can help busy people avoid standing in line. For example, Sierra and her coworkers have decided to order lunch from Wally's Super Subs. Using the office fax machine, Sierra places the lunch order at 11:00 a.m. Wally and his crew get the order from their fax machine. They prepare the food. When Sierra arrives at noon, the order is ready. She enjoys her lunch hour without waiting in line.

Because of the cost, fax machines are generally purchased for business rather than home use. If you need to use a fax machine for your personal business, you can go to an office service store that has fax machines available for public use.

When Not to Fax

Sometimes sending a fax is not practical or wise. Before you send a resume for a potential job, ask the business if you may fax your resume. Faxing a resume is not unusual. In fact, you may have noticed in help-wanted advertisements that some employers ask applicants to fax their resumes. Others may not want their fax machines tied up receiving resumes. They may prefer to keep their fax lines open for their regular business clients.

Faxing a very long document should be avoided. Documents longer than 12 pages should be delivered in a different way if possible. Ideally, a faxed document is only one page long.

You need to think before you fax private information. Remember that very often businesses located their fax machines in a centralized area of their offices. If the receiver does not immediately pick up the fax you sent, many people might read the fax without your knowledge. Before faxing, ask yourself, "Do I want others seeing this information?" If you must fax private information, call the person before you send the fax. Then the person can be at the fax machine and get it immediately.

A fax should not be used to avoid talking to someone face-to-face. For example, if you are quitting your job, you need to talk to your supervisor directly. It is not right to fax your resignation.

A Fax Cover Sheet

A fax cover sheet is a short form containing information about the fax and its sender. The cover sheet helps both the sender and the receiver because it is a record of the fax as well as a way to make sure that the complete information has been received. A cover sheet should always be sent with a fax.

To: *Howard Higgins*   **From:** *Twila James*

Organization: *Milo Junior College*

Telephone No.: *(768) 567-2000*   **Telephone No.:** *(345) 987-6700*

Fax Number: *(345) 987-6701*   **Fax Number:** *(768) 567-2001*

Date: *August 15, 2001*   **Number of Pages including cover:** *3*

Subject: *Grade Transcript*

Message: *I am faxing the unofficial grade transcript of Skyler Towns. The official transcript will be mailed next week.*

Cover Sheet Information

Some businesses use a standard fax form. Although not all fax cover sheets look the same, the basic information provided on the sheets is the same.

A cover sheet should include the name of the receiver. Remember that there may be more than one Richard in the office. So be sure to use both the first and last names. If the fax is being sent to a particular organization or company, the group's name should be written on the cover sheet. The telephone number as well as the fax number of the recipient should also be recorded.

You should include your complete name, telephone number, and fax number on the cover sheet. This provides a way for the receiver to immediately contact you if the fax doesn't come through or if it is incomplete.

The date needs to be recorded. If the person getting the fax is out of the office when the transmission occurs, knowing when the information was faxed may be important.

Be sure to record how many pages are being faxed. Notice that the number of pages includes the cover sheet. Sometimes a fax transmission is interrupted. Not all of the pages are transmitted. If this happens, the recipient can contact the sender, and another fax can be sent.

The subject line gives a short description of what is being faxed. Using the subject line lets the recipient verify that he has received the correct fax.

The message space allows the sender to add any additional information about the fax.

Check It Out 8-1

Use the information in each situation to fill out the fax cover sheet.

Situation No. 1: Nita Norris, a toy store manager, placed an order with Max Woods of The Toy Factory on April 1. Today is April 27. The order has not arrived. Using her fax number, (424) 233-3742, Nita will send Max a five-page copy of the original order form. She wants Max to make sure that the order has been sent. Nita's phone number is (424) 233-3743. The Toy Factory's phone number is (213) 789-2300. The fax number is (213) 789-2301.

To:	From:
Organization:	
Telephone No.:	Telephone No.:
Fax Number:	Fax Number:
Date:	Number of Pages Including cover:
Subject:	
Message:	

Situation No. 2: Sierra Martin is ordering lunch from Wally's Super Sub. She plans to pick it up at noon. Today is October 14. Using the office fax number, (913) 557-4142, she will send a one-page lunch order. Her phone number is (913) 557-4143. Wally's phone number is (913) 557-2381. The fax number is (913) 557-2382.

To:	From:
Organization:	
Telephone No.:	Telephone No.:
Fax Number:	Fax Number:
Date:	Number of Pages Including cover:
Subject:	
Message:	

Situation No. 3: On February 18, Marty Roth is sending a four-page document making an offer to purchase a house at 2804 Sea Breeze Lane in Tampa, Florida. His phone number is (602) 814-6534. His fax number is (602) 814-6535. The offer is being made through the Simmons Realty Company. The fax number is (703) 576-1231. The phone number is (703) 576-1232. Guy Simmons is the Realtor.

To:	From:
Organization:	
Telephone No.:	Telephone No.:
Fax Number:	Fax Number:
Date:	Number of Pages including cover:
Subject:	
Message:	

Situation No. 4: Morgan Miles is going out of town next week. She works for Southern Resorts. Her area supervisor, Gloria Hiatt, needs to know her traveling schedule for the week. Morgan's fax number is (456) 908-6789. She will fax her two-page schedule to Gloria (456) 657-8900. Today is September 28. Morgan's phone number is (456) 908-6790. Gloria's phone number is (456) 657-8901.

To:	From:
Organization:	
Telephone No.:	Telephone No.:
Fax Number:	Fax Number:
Date:	Number of Pages including cover:
Subject:	
Message:	

Faxing Clearly

Receiving a fax that is impossible to read is frustrating. When you send a fax, make sure that it is clear. Follow these simple rules to ensure that a readable fax is delivered:

● Be neat. If you are handwriting the material to be faxed, write clearly. Make sure that the print is dark and contrasts well with the lighter background. If you are using printed material, use a clean copy. Black or red ink transmit best. If you have made fluid corrections on the copy, make a photocopy of it before you fax it.

● Use an easy-to-read typeface, generally not less than 12 point. Use the same typeface for the entire fax.

● Don't squeeze the print together. Leave enough white space to make the fax easy to read. Leave large margins especially at the top and bottom of the pages.

● Keep the information brief. When you are writing, get to the point. If at all possible, limit the fax to one page.

● Limit graphics. Graphics take longer to transmit.

● Don't fax a fax. It will not transmit clearly.

● Before you fax the material, make sure that you have included all the information needed.

What Is E-mail?

Electronic mail (e-mail) is a non-verbal, written form of communication. Writing an e-mail message is very much like using a word processor to write. The difference is that an e-mail message can be sent to an individual without using paper and a printer. An e-mail message goes directly to an individual's computer. To both send and receive e-mail messages, a computer must be equipped with e-mail capabilities. Both the sender and the recipient need their own e-mail addresses.

Why Is E-mail Popular?

E-mail is a very popular form of communication. Businesses use e-mail frequently. Whole families use e-mail for corresponding. E-mail has become popular for many reasons:

● **E-mail is fast.** A post card sent via airmail from Japan will arrive in the United States at least one week after it is mailed. An e-mailed message sent today from Japan will arrive today.

● **E-mail can save time.** Using e-mail to correspond within a business means that workers aren't constantly interrupted with telephone calls. People trying to reach each other can avoid playing telephone tag throughout the workday.

- **E-mail is convenient.** E-mail can be sent from the office or from home. You do not need to buy stamps or drop the message into a mailbox. E-mail can take the place of expensive long-distance telephone calls.

- **E-mail is not limited by time zones.** Dealing with different time zones when you are corresponding by telephone can be very frustrating. Time zones mean nothing when e-mail is used. You may send an e-mail message at any time day or night. Your correspondent's system will receive the e-mail. Your message will be stored until your friend decides to check his e-mail messages.

- **After an e-mail message has been read, it can be stored for further reference.** You can file the information without a lot of paper lying around.

- **E-mail is not limited by distance or costs.** E-mail can be sent to the next office or to the other side of the world. Sending e-mails costs the same day or night and on weekends, too.

- **E-mail is an informal way of communicating.** Messages are short. An e-mail message does not have the formal form of a business letter. It is useful for distributing simple information quickly and easily.

- **E-mail is more like a conversation than any other type of written communication.** E-mail lets you keep in touch with your far-away friends and family.

The Disadvantages of E-mail

While e-mail is very convenient, it is not always the best form of corresponding. In some situations, another form of correspondence needs to be used:

- **E-mail is impersonal.** E-mail lacks personal contact. You cannot see or hear the other individual to interpret what is being said. Facial expressions, body language, and voice inflection help you understand fully what a speaker means. Emotional situations need to be handled face-to-face. If you are negotiating a problem, e-mail is not the best form of correspondence.

- **E-mail is not private.** Don't use e-mail when you are dealing with a personal topic. E-mail may appear unfriendly or intimidating to some people. Using the telephone or having a conversation is a better way to deal with others in this situation.

  Think about what you are e-mailing before you send it. Sometimes an e-mail is mistakenly sent to the wrong person. The message could be forwarded by the receiver. It could be printed and left in the printer. A computer may keep copies of e-mail. Don't e-mail information that you don't want others to see.

- **E-mail is brief.** E-mail is short. It is not useful for answering a long list of questions. It is awkward to use when communicating with a group of people. When a message is long or complex, another form of communication is more practical.

- **E-mail is easily ignored.** If you need an answer to a question right away, e-mail is not the best form of communication. The receiver may not check her e-mail before you need the answer, or she may get busy and not answer right away. If you need an immediate answer, use the telephone or talk to the person face-to-face.

Do You Have an E-mail Address?

Before you can send or receive e-mail, you must have an e-mail address. Here is the e-mail address of a familiar character:

unclesam@aol.com

Notice that the address is written in lowercase letters. An e-mail address has three parts:

1. The first part is the user's name. It may actually be the person's name or some other name the user chooses. In the example, it is **unclesam**.

2. The second part is the domain. The domain name follows the @. The domain is the computer or the network of computers where the address is stored. The domain in the example is **aol**.

3. The last part is the top-level domain name. In the example, **.com** is the top-level domain name. Some other top-level domain names are

   .org—organization

   .gov—government

   .edu—education

   .mil—military

   .net—network

   .int—international

Sending an E-mail

Using the e-mail format on your computer will help you remember what information is needed to send your e-mail message. By filling in the necessary information, your e-mail will be more easily understood.

Header

The first part of an e-mail is called the header. It includes information that is needed to deliver the e-mail, including the e-mail address of the user, the address of the recipient, and a brief description of the message being sent.

Sample E-mail Header

When you get ready to compose an e-mail, your e-mail address will automatically appear on the "From:" line. Your computer will provide the day, date, and time on the "date line."

> **From:** unclesam@aol.com
>
> **Sent Sunday, April 15, 2001 9:15 a.m.**
>
> **To:** maryellens@indy.net
>
> **cc:** mulligan49@purdue.edu
>
> **Subject: Tax Tips**

You will need to supply the other information. You may type in the e-mail address on the "To:" line, or you may go to your address book to get it. A computerized address book lists e-mail addresses you use often.

Before sending the e-mail, check the receiver's address. Make sure it is typed correctly. E-mail addresses are written in lowercase letters and have no blank spaces. Any blank spaces should be filled by using either an underscore (_) or a dot (.). Never use quotation marks around an e-mail address.

You may want to send a carbon copy (cc) or a blind carbon copy (Bcc) to another person. This is a copy of your e-mail, sent to a second person. A blind carbon copy is sent to a second person without the first recipient's knowledge. If you want a copy of an e-mail sent to another person, you must type that person's e-mail address on the cc or Bcc line. Be careful not to make carbon copies if you know the first person getting your message doesn't want others to see it.

Sometimes an e-mail will "bounce" back to the sender. This means the e-mail could not be delivered as it was addressed. If this happens to you, check the recipient's address. You may have made a mistake in copying the e-mail or used the wrong e-mail address.

The Subject Line

The subject line briefly describes the reason you are sending the message. It may also be called the message line, the topic, or "Re:" (for "regarding").

For people who get a lot of e-mail, the subject line is a big help. It allows them to browse through their e-mail directories and decide what needs to be read first. If you leave this line blank, a busy person may just ignore your message.

The subject line should be short and to the point. Don't be vague by just saying "Information." Be more specific such as "Information about Weekend Camping Trip." It doesn't need to be a complete sentence. When you are writing, use either all lowercase or both uppercase and lowercase letters. Since a lot of junk mail uses all uppercase letters, the reader may just ignore messages written that way. Plus, words written in all uppercase letters in an e-mail are considered a form of rude "shouting" at the reader.

If your message needs to be read right away, you might use the word "Urgent" in the subject line. The letters "FYI" (for your information) indicate a non-urgent message. If you are sending a really long message, you may warn the reader by saying in the subject line "Long message."

The Body

The body is simply what you want to say in the e-mail. It may also be called the message, the text, or your words.

Do not use complicated words and phrases when writing an e-mail. Keep it brief and to the point. An e-mail message should be clear enough that the reader understands its purpose.

An e-mail message should stand on its own. In other words, the reader should not have to refer to another e-mail to understand the current message. For example, an e-mail you sent to Sid last week suggested that the two of you meet on Tuesday or Wednesday of this week. Sid e-mailed you today saying he will meet you, but he doesn't say which day.

Don't e-mail him saying, "Sid, which day?" He may have forgotten the days. Instead, e-mail Sid saying, "Sid, which day—Tuesday or Wednesday?"

Your system may allow you to add an attachment to your e-mail. Perhaps you have a document that you want to send along with the e-mail message. It is possible to attach the document to the e-mail and send it as well.

The Signature Line

The signature line is the final part of the e-mail. Your computer automatically places your e-mail address on the "From:" line at the top of the e-mail form. But you may still want to use the signature because your e-mail address may not use your full name. Using the signature line also indicates the end of the e-mail.

In an informal e-mail, the signature may just be the person's first name. In a business situation, it may include the person's full name, a title, an e-mail address, and even a telephone number. Some people use a feature on their computer that automatically puts the signature at the end of the e-mail.

© JIST Works, Indianapolis, IN

Forwarding E-mail

You can send an e-mail message that you have received to another person. This is called forwarding. To do this, you must click on "forward" and supply the correct e-mail address. Forwarding is a great convenience because you do not have to retype the information.

✓ Check It Out   8-2

Fill in the following information about e-mail.

1. List five reasons that e-mail is so popular in today's world.

   _____

   _____

   _____

   _____

   _____

2. List three times when using e-mail would not be the best choice.

   _____

   _____

   _____

3. How does the subject line help the person receiving an e-mail?

   _____

   _____

   _____

4. What information must the user provide in the header of an e-mail?

   _____

   _____

   _____

5. Why are the cc and Bcc lines used?

   _____

   _____

   _____

(continues)

6. What feature would a user need to send an e-mail from one friend to another friend?

_____

_____

_____

7. What should you do if an e-mail "bounces" back to you?

_____

_____

_____

8. What is meant by the statement "An e-mail should stand on its own."?

_____

_____

_____

9. Why should the signature line be written at the end of an e-mail?

_____

_____

_____

10. List some different information that the signature line may include.

_____

_____

_____

E-mail Style

E-mail messages are brief and written to be read quickly. The writing in an e-mail should be simple and natural. Write like you talk, but organize your thoughts to keep the message short.

Paragraphs should be short. Double space between paragraphs. You can use lists in e-mails to emphasize points or show the steps needed to accomplish something.

Write in complete sentences. Both proper spelling and grammar should be used in e-mail.

Before sending an e-mail, read the message. Make sure it can be understood. Check the spelling, grammar, and punctuation.

E-mail Etiquette

Always remember that your e-mail might be read by others, not just the person you are e-mailing. Sometimes e-mails even get posted. Think before you send an e-mail. If you feel angry or especially emotional, wait before sending an e-mail.

Be thoughtful of others' privacy. Don't give out others' e-mail addresses without their permission. Before forwarding someone else's e-mail, make sure you have his permission to do it.

Read and answer your e-mail. Get in the habit of checking your e-mail.

Be careful how you write an e-mail. It is very easy for a reader to misunderstand sarcasm and humor used in an e-mail because the speaker can't use facial expressions or voice inflections to convey "I'm just kidding." Reread an e-mail before sending it.

Check Your Vocabulary

A	address book	I	subject line
B	cc	J	e-mail address
C	fax machine	K	body
D	header	L	attachment
E	"bounce"	M	fax number
F	e-mail	N	Bcc
G	signature	O	forward
H	fax cover sheet		

1. _____ A person's computerized list of frequently used e-mail addresses.

2. _____ The method used to send a copy of an e-mail message you have received to a third person.

3. _____ To return an e-mail to the sender when it can't be delivered.

4. _____ A document or other information that is added to an e-mail message for delivery.

5. _____ The part of an e-mail containing the e-mail addresses of the sender and recipient, a brief description of the message being sent, as well as the date and time.

6. _____ Carbon copy; a way to send a copy of your e-mail message to a third person without retyping it.

7. _____ The last item in an e-mail; lets the receiver know that the e-mail is finished.

8. _____ The first page of a fax giving information about the recipient and sender, the length of the fax, and the reason for the fax.

9. _____ Blind carbon copy; sending a copy of your e-mail to a second person without telling the first recipient person.

10. _____ A mechanism that translates written words into electrical signals that are transmitted through a telephone line to a similar machine. The second machine prints the words and makes a copy of the original document.

11. _____ The information needed to send electronic mail to a person or organization; the user's name, domain, and top-level domain.

12. _____ The area code, prefix, and 4-digit number needed to send a fax message.

13. _____ The message or the text of an e-mail.

14. _____ Electronic mail.

15. _____ A brief description of an e-mail message.

Summing It Up

In today's world, knowing how to use technological communication is extremely important. Using a fax machine makes getting documents into the hands of another person across the country fast and easy. E-mail is not limited by time or distance.

The way we communicate changes constantly. Each of us needs to be aware of those changes and continue to learn how to use new technology. Knowing how to use all types and means of communication will make you effective in both your personal and work worlds.